How to Start a Life Science Company

A Comprehensive Guide for First-Time Entrepreneurs

by Leah Cannon

This publication has been written to provide accurate information in regard to the subject matter covered. It does not provide legal, regulatory, financial, tax or accounting advice. All startup entrepreneurs should consult the appropriate experts as required.

First published in 2017

ISBN-10: 0-6481423-2-9
ISBN-13: 978-0-6481423-2-4

To K.C.
For your invaluable help with this book
and your very valued friendship.

Table of Contents

Introduction

Scientists, engineers and healthcare professionals usually have very little business training. Therefore, if you make an exciting new discovery or have a brilliant idea on how to improve patient care, it can be very difficult to know how to turn that discovery or idea into a successful business.

Life science encompasses the biotech, medtech, digital health and healthcare sectors. Our industry is highly regulated because we develop products and services that affect people's health. Life science entrepreneurs across all sectors face challenges that other entrepreneurs don't face, including intellectual property (IP) ownership and protection, regulatory compliance, and long and expensive product development cycles. If you make your discovery while working at a university or research institute, you may not even own your work. Raising funding is another major challenge for life science entrepreneurs. Investors are understandably wary of startup companies, particularly of biotech startups. Nine out of ten startups fail. Less than 10% of Phase I clinical trial candidates are approved by the FDA.

I am a scientist and a veterinarian and so know first-hand how difficult it can be to assimilate into the startup world. It's a whole new language and way of thinking. Since leaving the bench, I have worked as a freelance marketing consultant for startup companies and life science organizations. In this role, I have spoken and worked with hundreds of life science entrepreneurs. I am always struck by the similarities between their stories. Entrepreneurs with many different kinds of technologies and products - from diagnostics to oral vaccines to software that aids with clinical diagnosis of back pain - tell me the same things. They have a sort of blueprint of how a clinician or a scientist could found a successful life science company.

So, I decided to take this advice, along with a lot of research, and turn it into this book: a how-to guide for scientists, engineers, healthcare professionals and students who want to start a life science company. It covers the business basics that we didn't have time to learn at university. All terms that show up in bold are included in a glossary at the back of the book. At the end of each chapter, I've also listed references and further resources, most of which are freely available, to help you on your entrepreneurship journey. All dollar values throughout this book are in US dollars.

Chapter One:
Analyze Your Science

Not all science can or should be commercialized. If you are a new entrepreneur, or a scientist thinking about becoming an entrepreneur, it isn't always easy to work out whether research could be turned into a successful business.

Here are the basic steps to turn science into a product:

- Idea or discovery
- Market research
- Protect intellectual property
- Decide on application
- Prototype or preclinical testing
- Clinical testing
- Regulatory approval
- Market

It takes years and millions of dollars to turn those steps into reality. How can you decide whether it is worthwhile spending the time and money trying to commercialize a particular technology?

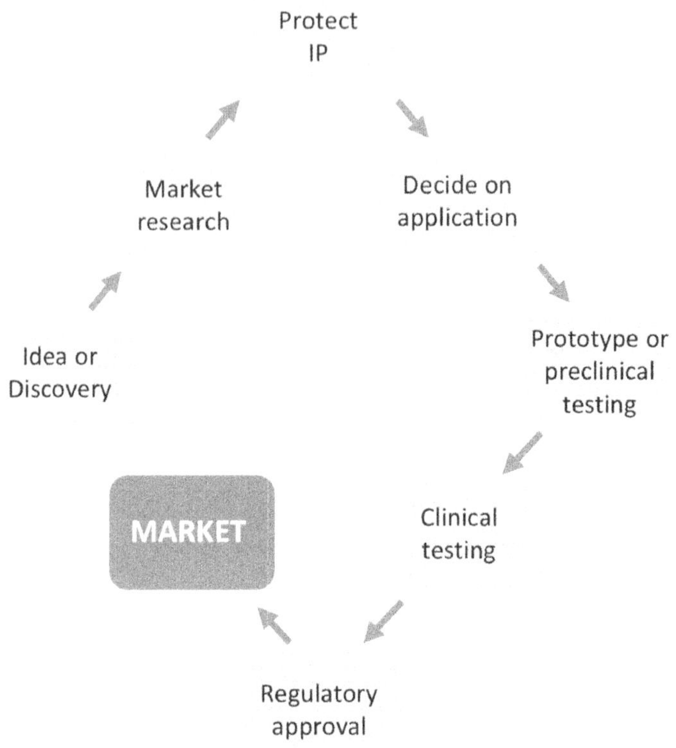

Figure 1.1 The commercialization cycle

If you work or study at a university or research institution, your Technology Transfer Office (TTO) can help you with this. In fact, you have to let them drive the commercialization process. Since the **Bayh-Dole Act** was passed in 1980, universities and non-profit research institutes in the US own any technology arising from federally-funded research at their facilities. This law requires universities and institutes to patent any useful inventions that they own and to license that technology to interested commercial partners. In Europe, many universities and research institutes have similar intellectual property rights in place.

If your work was sponsored by a company through a **Sponsored Research Agreement** or contract, the sponsoring company may have the first right to refuse licensing any resulting IP or they may have a time window in which they can negotiate to license any technology.

Some institutions claim ownership of discoveries coming from *any* work done by their employees, regardless of where it was done, so make sure you check your employment contract before doing work in a Community Lab or other premises.

For any discoveries made at a university or research institution, report your IP to your TTO and they will assess the commerciality of your discovery and work with you on drafting patent claims. If they do decide to patent it, you may be able to negotiate later to license the technology back from them so you can commercialize it.

If you are a solo entrepreneur who invented your technology outside of a company or research organization, these are the steps to work out whether your technology can be commercialized:

- Who owns it? Was it derived from your previous job?
- How strong is the science?
- Can you defend your IP and how will you do so?
- What products, platforms or services can you create from your science?
- Is there a market need for these applications?
- What is your market size?
- Who are your competitors?
- How difficult/expensive will it be to develop these applications?

Do you own it?

Ownership of a scientific invention comes down to three things: who did the work; where the work took place and who paid for it. If you did the work in an independent lab space such as a community lab, incubator or accelerator and you paid for it, then you are the owner.

To stay away from sticky ownership fights, make sure you read the fine print in any contract you sign with an independent lab. If they don't have a clear ownership policy or contract, you might want to draft one and ask them to sign it. Also use **Material Transfer Agreements** (MTAs) if using materials from collaborators or other researchers. These should clearly state who is using what and who owns any IP resulting from the use of these materials.

If you are still working at a university or research institution while doing your independent work, you may need to sign a consulting agreement with them to be sure that they don't have an ownership claim to any of your IP. Whether or not this is possible depends on the source of your funding and varies from institution to institution so check with your TTO or your human resources department. Also, if you are an expat working on a visa, you have to follow different rules, so check out the rules specific to your visa before you spend time and money on creating independent work. You may not be allowed to do so under your visa regulations.

> *"If you don't have that letter, your university could come after you."*
>
> ***Naresh Sunkara, former postdoc, now CEO of Nosocom Solutions***

You may be able to ask your institution for a **non-assert letter** stating they will not contest ownership of your IP. Naresh Sunkara developed the technology for his company Nosocom Solutions while he was a postdoc at the University of California, Berkeley. He did his work at independent facilities outside of the university. He told Berkeley what he was doing and they wrote a letter for him starting that the university had no ownership rights over his technology.

How strong is the science?

Pharmaceutical companies conduct research in a very different way from most academic labs. Their end goal is to create products and platforms. This means that all research must be well documented and reproducible. Otherwise the company could spend millions or billions of dollars and many years running down dead-end paths. Companies want to get to a '**go/no-go decision**' as fast as possible to save time and money. They are biased towards no. Academic labs on the other hand, are often trying to find new knowledge, not create products. They are biased towards yes.

> ***Go/No-Go Decisions***
>
> *Entrepreneurs must constantly assess whether they are developing the right product or application and building the right business to be profitable. These are called 'go/no-go' decisions.*
>
> *It may be that after market sizing, you realize that there isn't a big enough market for your product to justify the time and expense it would take to develop it. This is a very difficult realization for an entrepreneur to make, but it is much better to arrive at this 'no-go' decision before you have invested four years and $100,000 of your own money in the project.*

As basic research funding dwindles, many universities and institutions are moving towards 'translational research' so many more academic researchers will need to think about how their work can be turned into products.

If you want to go down the harrowing road of spinning out a startup company based on your research, you need to know that the science is solid. *This is one of the first questions that early stage investors will ask.* They want to know that you have novel technology that can be used to make a product that solves a problem for a big market.

Peer review of your work can provide some external validation of your science. Securing grant funding, winning business competitions and being accepted into an incubator or accelerator program all involve peer review of your science.

If you are still at the earliest stage of your entrepreneurship journey, and haven't yet had the chance to apply for grants or enter competitions, you need to objectively assess the quality of your science. It might help to ask a couple of colleagues to do this, particularly if they are well known in your field. These same colleagues may write you letters of support to strengthen your grant applications or investment pitch.

Investors will analyze your data themselves. They will look at the robustness of any patents and academic publications. They will also assess the strength of your scientific advisory board.

Can you defend your IP?

The best way to protect IP is to apply for a patent. Investors prefer to invest in life science companies that own patented technology, rather than those that rely on trade secrets to protect their IP. However, not all ideas and technologies are patentable. For example, software is very difficult, if not impossible to patent.

You can only patent and defend IP that is 'new' (more on this in Chapter Two). That means you cannot publicly disclose or publish your work in any way before applying for a patent. If in doubt, ask a patent lawyer or TTO.

To work out whether your technology is 'new', you will need to do a **patent analysis**. This means searching the US Patent Office database, and equivalent databases in other countries, as well as all published scientific literature and conference proceedings, to check whether similar technology has already been patented for the same applications.

Patent applications are technical documents that can be difficult to understand without the help of a professional. Scientists and engineers are smart and used to learning quickly about new techniques and new fields. However, there are two areas in the product development pathway where life science entrepreneurs consistently recommend getting help and that is with IP protection and with regulatory compliance concerns.

If you are at a university or academic institute, your TTO will do a patent analysis for you or will work with patent lawyers to ensure that your technology is patentable. If you are a solo entrepreneur, it is worth speaking with a patent lawyer.

What products, platforms or services can you create from your science?

You can't sell science to customers. You have to sell a product, a platform or a service. Each of these is a different application of your technology.

Your science is commercially valuable only if you can turn it into one or more applications *that people will buy*. That last part is key. Even if your product or service is one of the most innovative things ever created, if people don't need it, you will find it almost impossible to sell.

The difference between a product, platform and service

*A **product** is a discrete stand-alone entity that people can buy or sell.*

*A **platform** is an ecosystem or a system that connects people or allows people to make products.*

*A **service** provides value or creates products for people.*

A company can choose to create any combination of products, services and platforms from its technology.

For example, a company with a novel RNA medicine delivery technology could develop a platform with which it tests and develops many different RNA medicines. Any medicines that pass through pre-clinical and clinical trials could then be sold as products. As a source of revenue, the company could also offer a service to other companies where it uses its drug discovery and development platform to develop RNA medicines for partner organizations.

Make a list of possible applications

Make a list of all the possible products, platforms and services that you could make from your technology. There will be some obvious ones but you also want to take the time to think about the less obvious options. This may help you to pivot and grow later as a company and realize the true value of your technology.

Search the internet for companies with similar technologies and see what they are developing. Ask co-workers to give you five possible applications. Talk to your TTO. Talk to entrepreneurs in your city, especially if there are any at your institution, and ask them, without giving away too many details, for potential applications. Investors are also very good at coming up with new ideas for technologies and can help you to pivot your entire company.

Rank all the applications you come up with in order of how easy or difficult they would be to make and how well they fill a market need or solve a problem that a large number of people have. There's a method to do this in the 'Viable Option' section below.

Non-Disclosure Agreements

If you want to share confidential details of your technology with any advisors, mentors or consultants, make sure they sign a non-disclosure agreement (NDA). You can easily find NDA templates on the internet.

Learn to pitch your technology and company without sharing confidential information. Professional investors will not sign an NDA before listening to a pitch. They see too many pitches.

Is there a market need for these applications?

The next step is to decide whether there is a true market need for each potential application. Ask yourself:

1. 'What problems does this product or service solve?'
2. 'Who has those problems?'
3. 'How do these potential customers currently solve those problems?'
4. 'How is my solution better?'

Customer interviews

If you don't create a product, platform or service that customers want, you will find it very difficult to build a successful business. The best way to avoid this is to go out and talk to potential customers.

If you are developing a therapeutic drug for an obvious unmet medical need with a big market, it is easy to believe that doctors and patients will want to use your product. However, you can still benefit from talking to doctors and asking them how they currently treat patients with this medical need and what their ideal treatment would be. You can also ask doctors what problems they have that you might be able to solve. You may be surprised to learn that your technology could be used to solve physicians' problems as well as patients' problems. You can also ask physicians what other problems their patients have and how they work to solve those problems.

> *"You may have the best technology that improves patient quality of life and compliance, but if you don't have buy-in from providers or payers, you have nothing."*
>
> ***Jon Wilensky, Board certified plastic surgeon and CEO of Braykion***

Speak with patients and ask them how they want to take their medicine. Would they be willing to inject a treatment three times a day, or use an inhaler several times a day or have a slow release capsule implanted under their skin? These conversations can teach you a lot about different formulations and preferred delivery systems as well as acceptable and unacceptable side effects in this patient population.

This is even more important if you are creating a medical device. Just because you think your medical device is better and faster than what is currently available, doesn't mean doctors will prescribe it or patients will use it and it definitely doesn't mean that insurance companies will pay for it.

You will learn a huge amount by talking to people. You will find out whether they would use the application you are thinking about creating, how they would use it, what other products or services they wish existed and much more. You can take all this information and use it to create the best product or service possible.

Customer interviews also give you the chance to start building relationships with potential customers. Some of these people may become your most loyal early adopters and help you to build your brand recognition even before you launch your first product or service. Invite key opinion leaders, particularly those working in prestigious hospitals and training the next generation of physicians, to join your scientific advisory board.

You can also ask potential customers and key opinion leaders—whether they are patients, doctors, patient advocacy groups, health insurance companies or hospitals—to write letters of support stating that they would buy your product or service if it were created. This will help you later when you are ready to look for investment.

Investors will speak to actual and potential customers when they are assessing your company and deciding whether or not to invest.

End-user or customer?

Be careful to distinguish between **end-users** and **customers**. Customers are the people who pay for your product or service and end-users are the people who use it. If you are creating a product or service that people use in a hospital, then the hospital is your customer and the patients are your end-users. Likewise, if your application will be used by people enrolled in a certain healthcare plan, the health insurance company is your customer and the employees are the end-users.

You should look to get input from both end-users and customers when designing and developing your applications.

Braykion is a startup company in San Diego developing a system to monitor handwashing in healthcare workers. Poor handwashing compliance causes 100,000 preventable deaths and costs $40 billion per year in the US alone. In Braykion's case, health care workers are the end-users. They wear Braykion's monitoring system. However, hospitals are the customers because they pay for the product.

Viable option list

Once you know there is a market for an application, you can put it into your 'viable option' list. To work out which application you should pursue first, you need to know which has the largest market, the fewest competitors and will be the quickest and easiest to design, test, manufacture and have approved by regulatory agencies. There may be no one application that scores best for all these parameters, but you can use a scoring system that takes all of them into account when you decide which application is most likely to be successful. Here is an example table that you could use:

Product Service or Platform	Market Size	Competitors	Product development timeline	Regulatory Route

What is your market size?

Market size is often called the **Total Addressable Market** or TAM. TAM is the revenue you would earn if you could reach 100% of your target market. However, TAM is not really your market size. Even with the most innovative technology and marketing plan, you will never reach 100% of any market.

The **available market** is the amount of the TAM that you can reach with your marketing. The **obtainable market** is the segment that will buy your application (Figure 1.2). That is your true market size. There is a general consensus among entrepreneurs that you need a market size of at least $1 billion to be able to attract angel or venture capital investment.

To work out the market size for each application on your viable option list, you need to do market analysis. This means understanding who is your customer, the number of these potential customers, how many of these people you can reach and how quickly you can reach them.

There are two ways to calculate market size: top down and bottom up. In the top down approach, you estimate the total dollar value spent on similar products. For example, if you are developing a spinal implant and $4 billion is spent each year on spinal implants worldwide, then your TAM is $4 billion. Your obtainable market is how much of that market will buy your implant rather than competing implants.

Figure 1.2 Market size graphic to use in pitch deck (insert relevant values)

In the bottom down approach, you calculate TAM by working out how many people need your product or service and multiplying this by the average sale price. In the example of spinal implants, you would work out how many people need spinal implants each year, then multiply that by the average sale price of each implant. Your obtainable market will depend on how many people will use your product instead of competing products. This is your **market penetrance** and depends on the visibility of your product *i.e.* how well you market it.

Market size = number of customers x penetrance x average sale value

To make this calculation, you need a rough idea of the average value of each sale of a 'unit' of your application. You'll need to factor in the estimated cost of production for your application as well as acceptable price points for your target customers. Customer interviews, customer personas and competitive analysis can help you work out these numbers. If you know a competitor drug sells for $5,000 per month, it is reasonable to predict that your drug could sell for at least that amount.

Building **customer personas** is big outside of the life science industry. It is more than just doing customer interviews. You also need to research their spending habits: their disposable income; what they purchase and how; the price bracket in which they will buy an equivalent product and their design preferences. Intuitively this appears to be less important in healthcare, as patients will want a new treatment or device that helps them better manage their disease. However, in many cases, the patients are the end-users, not the customers. Your customers, also called payers, are hospitals, insurance companies or national public healthcare systems like Medicare in Australia or the National Health Service (NHS) in the UK. It can be very helpful to work out how much insurance companies or healthcare systems spend on equivalent products and services.

You can do this by searching for **reimbursement** codes. These codes tell you what similar products have been covered by insurance companies or national healthcare programs and how much payers paid for these products. You can hire reimbursement consultants or agencies to help you with these searches. I go through reimbursement strategies in more detail in Chapter Four.

When calculating market size, you also need to work out the number of potential customers. You can search the scientific literature for disease prevalence and incidence and use census data and information from the World Health Organization and patient advocacy groups.

It can be much harder to estimate how many of these customers you can reach and how quickly you can do that. This depends on many factors, some of which you can control and some of which you can't. Depending on how much capital you have available, you can have a reasonable amount of control over your marketing, public relations and industry partnerships. All of these will help spread the word about your product or service. However, you can't control patient demographics such as income and health insurance status. Also, while you can work with regulatory and reimbursement experts while designing and developing your application to try and ensure that insurers and other payers will ultimately pay for your product or

> ***Reimbursement***
>
> *Reimbursement refers to whether a payer - a health insurance company or national healthcare system - will pay for your product or service. If payers will not cover your product, it will be very difficult to sell. Therefore, you need to know if payers have covered similar devices. You also need a reimbursement strategy to ensure that payers cover your product. More on this in Chapter Four.*

service, this is another factor that you cannot completely control.

Building best case and worse case scenarios for market size will help you decide whether or not to move forward with any of your viable options. Making a list of all the risks involved at each step and of the assumptions you have made in your calculations will also help.

Note: Keep watch on the total addressable, available and obtainable markets throughout your product development pipeline and beyond. These can change over time which may have a devastating effect on your business. Also keep an eye on competitors. New ones will pop up all the time.

Who are your competitors?

The next step is to analyze your competitors. How many of them are there? Who are they and how are their applications different and similar to yours? This will help you understand your **point of difference** or **unique selling point** *i.e.* what makes you better than your competitors.

Don't show a big competitive analysis table in your investor pitch – show it in a graph or matrix.

Who your competitors are will depend on both your technology and your application. If you are developing a new therapeutic for lymphoma then all other companies creating lymphoma therapeutics are **direct competitors**. But what about companies developing therapeutics for other cancers? Could any of these also be used to treat lymphoma? Are there any companies creating medical devices to either help treat or diagnose lymphoma? What about companies developing medical devices or diagnostics for other cancers? Does anyone have a cancer diagnosis platform? These could be **indirect competitors**. For example, if a new drug is initially approved to treat leukemia but subsequent trials show it is also effective in treating lymphoma, then this company would then become a direct competitor.

It can be very difficult to find out about new biotech and life science companies. Many operate 'under the radar' while they are in preclinical development. However, you can look at the product pipelines of large and mid-sized pharmaceutical and biotech companies as well as any smaller companies with websites. There are also many company aggregators like Crunchbase and AngelList that you can use to search for competitors.

Make a table or a list with each potential competitor, their products, the mode of action (MOA) of each product and the price of each product.

Competitor	Product	MOA	Price	Strengths	Weaknesses

How are you different? Are you developing a drug with a new mode of action to treat this disease? That is called **first-in-class**. Or are you developing a drug or device that works in a similar way to the market leader but has better pharmacokinetics or performance? This is called **best-in-class**. Or does your platform allow new medicines to be produced significantly more quickly or cheaply than competitors? This would give you a **price advantage**.

Each of these points of difference comes with its own risks. If you are aiming for first-in-class, your drug mechanism will never have been tested in your target patient population. So, there is a good chance that the drug will fail clinical trials. If you are going for best-in-class, then there will be more data showing that similar drugs do work in your patient population but your drug may not outperform these similar drugs. Or insurance companies and payers may not choose to pay for your drug instead of the old drug.

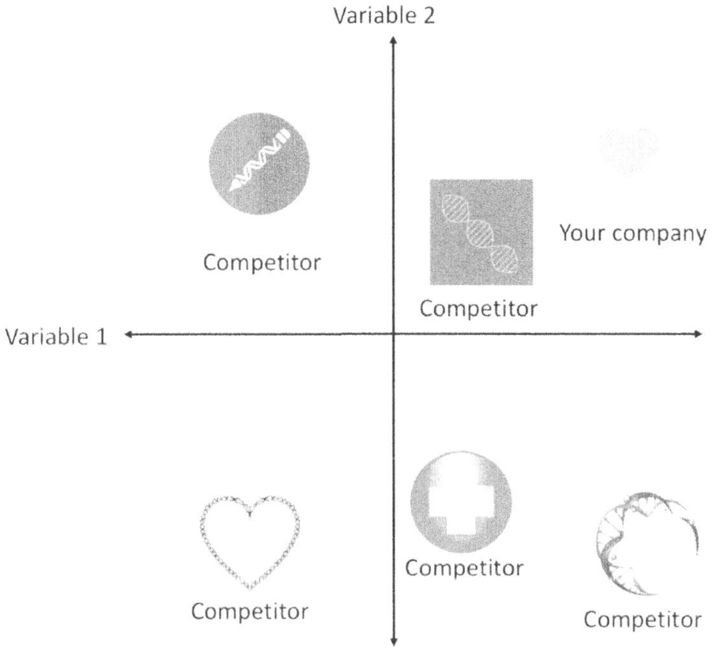

Figure 1.3 Example of competitive analysis graph

Competitive analysis is not only important as a tool to help you decide which application of your technology you should develop first, it is also an essential part of any pitch to investors. Investors don't need to see every single potential competitor, at least in your initial pitch, but they do need to know that you know about every competitor and you know how you are different and why you are better. It will also help you work out appropriate pricing for your application and put a dollar value on your company when you are ready to look for investment.

When creating your pitch deck, you can show your competitive analysis as a graph like Figure 1.3, or if you want to show more than two variables, use a matrix like Figure 1.4.

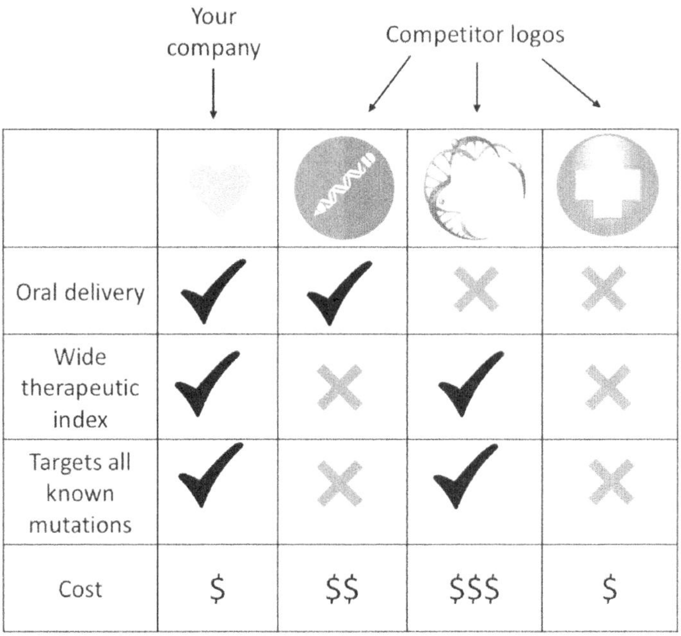

Figure 1.4 Competitive analysis matrix to include in pitch deck

Note: Just like with market analysis, you want to keep up to date with what your competitors are doing and regularly check for new competitors.

Product development plan

The US Food and Drug Administration (FDA) divides the healthcare product development process into five stages: Discovery and Development; Preclinical Research; Clinical Research; FDA Review and Post-Market Safety and Monitoring.

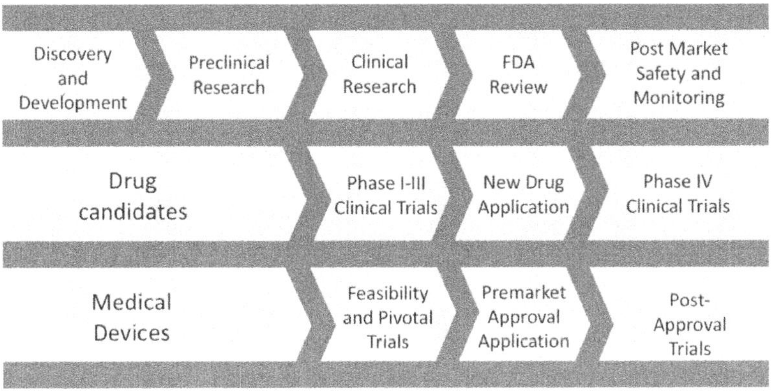

Figure 1.5 Life science product development pathway in the US

Although all products will need to pass through these five stages, your specific product development and regulatory pathway will depend on whether you are developing a pharmaceutical, a medical device, equipment, consumables or software. It will also depend on whether you are seeking regulatory approval in the US, Europe or other countries. All regulatory agencies, including the FDA and the European Medicines Agency (EMA) have specific guidelines and these must be met in order to receive approval. You can find out a lot of information from regulatory agency websites. However, when it comes time to plan your preclinical research, you can ensure that you have the right experimental design by consulting with a regulatory affairs expert.

I go through regulatory pathways in the US and Europe in Chapter Three and product development plans in Chapter Four.

Marketing plan

You will need an in-depth marketing plan when you start pitching to investors. This will form part of your business plan. At the early product analysis stage, when you are building your viable option list, you should have an idea of who your customers are and how will you get to them. You should also try to come up with a ball park figure of how much this would cost and how this would differ for the possible applications of your technology. I will go through marketing plans in more detail in Chapter Twelve.

Further resources

Here are some free online resources where you can find more information about the concepts outlined in this chapter.

Bayh-Dole Act: https://grants.nih.gov/grants/bayh-dole.htm

FDA Resources on Drugs and Devices: https://clinicaltrials.gov/ct2/info/fdalinks

MARS: How to Estimate Market Size: https://www.marsdd.com/mars-library/how-to-estimate-market-size-business-and-marketing-planning-for-startups/

Chapter Two: Protect Your Intellectual Property

This chapter outlines some of the intellectual property (IP) protection concerns faced by biotech entrepreneurs. It does not offer legal advice. IP protection is key to building a successful life science company. While entrepreneurs can bootstrap and DIY many things, I highly recommend you seek professional help for IP protection, and do it earlier rather than later. If your IP is not adequately protected, investors will not invest in your company, regulatory agencies will not approve your products and pharmaceutical and larger biotech companies will not license your technologies or acquire your company.

Don't talk about it

If you disclose your technology to the public in any way, and this can include publishing an academic article, presenting at a conference or research institution or writing about your technology on a lab or personal blog, you may not be able to patent it. For a patent application to be approved by the US Patent and Trademark Office (USPTO) or the European Patent Office, the invention must be 'new'. To establish whether the invention or idea is truly novel, the relevant patent office will compare it to all '**prior art**', which is everything that has been published or publicly disclosed before the patent application was submitted.

The America Invents Act, which was passed in 2013, changed the rules slightly so that publications and disclosures by the inventor about his or her work are not be counted as prior art if they occur within 12 months of filing the patent application. However, this is not the case in any other countries around the world. Therefore, to be on the safe side, it is a much better policy not to share any information about any IP you think you might want to patent.

Much of the best science comes from collaboration. Working with other scientists doesn't mean you can't protect your IP. If you need to share materials with either individual researchers or research organizations, use a Material Transfer Agreement (MTA): a contract stating the terms of the material transfer and the rights of each party. If you need to share information with collaborators or contractors, use a Non-Disclosure Agreement (NDA), also called a Confidential Disclosure Agreement (CDA).

You can protect your IP by filing for a **patent** or keeping it as a **trade secret**. If you need to use IP owned by other parties, even if it is technology that you invented but is owned by your university or research institution, you will need to secure a **license** that gives you the right to use that technology.

You can also use a **trademark** to protect your company name and any product names and use **copyright** to protect any written work such as white papers.

Patents

The USPTO defines a patent as "the right to exclude others from making, using, offering for sale, or selling the invention in the United States or importing the invention into the United States." A patent may be granted to prevent others from commercializing a device, substance, method or process that is **new**, **non-obvious** and **useful**.

Likewise, the European Patent Office states that an invention can only be patented if it is "new, industrially applicable and involve(s) an inventive step."

When talking about patents, the words new, non-obvious and useful are legal terms with specific definitions.

An invention will not be considered new by US patent law if:

> *"(1) the claimed invention was patented, described in a printed publication, or in public use, on sale, or otherwise available to the public before the effective filing date of the claimed invention" or*
> *"(2) the claimed invention was described in a patent issued [by the U.S.] or in an application for patent published or deemed published [by the U.S.], in which the patent or application, as the case may be, names another inventor and was effectively filed before the effective filing date of the claimed invention."*

'Otherwise available to the public' is an important clause. It means that if you share information about your technology or invention in any form, including at a conference or institutional meeting, you will not be able to patent it. Any mention of your technology in any form is called 'prior art' and will negate your right to patent your technology.

The term of most US and European patents is 20 years from the date of filing. With the exception of European patents, which may cover all countries in the European Patent Convention (more below), you need to apply for a patent in each country where you wish to manufacture or sell your product.

Patent Cooperation Treaty (PCT)

Unfortunately, there is no international or worldwide patent. There is, however, the **Patent Cooperation Treaty (PCT)**, which is an agreement between 152 countries. The PCT allows you to file one international patent application that simultaneously seeks patent protection in any or all of the 152 countries that have signed the treaty (these countries are called contracting states).

When you file an international patent application, an International Searching Authority will then search databases worldwide for patent documents or published technical and scientific literature with any evidence of prior art *i.e.* any mention of your technology. This includes any published patent applications in any country. Therefore, if you are based in the US and may wish to sell your product or service in other countries, *you must file an international patent application at the same time as your US patent application*. Seek professional advice from a patent lawyer on the specific timing and number of patents that you will need to protect your IP and be able to execute your business plan.

European Patents

You can apply for one European patent which will cover any or all of the 38 countries that are members of the European Patent Convention (EPC).

EPC countries are: Albania, Austria, Belgium, Bulgaria, Croatia, Cyprus, Czech Republic, Denmark, Estonia, Finland, France, Germany, Greece, Hungary, Iceland, Ireland, Italy, Latvia, Liechtenstein, Lithuania,

Luxembourg, Macedonia, Malta, Monaco, Netherlands, Norway, Poland, Portugal, Romania, San Marino, Serbia, Slovakia, Slovenia, Spain, Sweden, Switzerland, Turkey and United Kingdom.

European patent applications must be filed in English at the European Patent Office.

Provisional Patents

In the US and Australia, you can apply for a provisional patent before submitting a full patent application. It is quicker, easier and cheaper than applying for a full patent and will help you to establish a **priority date**, which is the official date from which you are legally recognized as having the right to exclude others from using and commercializing your technology.

However, your provisional patent application must be scientifically rigorous and cover all of the intended uses of your technology that you want to protect (your **claims**). Also, you must submit a full patent application within 12 months of filing your provisional patent application. If you submit a poorly worded provisional patent application, it may jeopardize your chances of having your full patent application accepted.

Licenses

In some cases, you will need to use someone else's technology to develop and commercialize your own tech. If that technology has been patented, you will need a license from the owner giving you the right to use their technology. Make sure this license is very well documented and kept at hand. Investors will ask to see it (after signing an NDA, of course).

There are three main types of license: **exclusive**, **sole** and **non-exclusive**. Licenses can also be world-wide or restricted to one or more countries. An exclusive license gives a licensee the exclusive rights to use the IP covered by the license. In the case of an exclusive license, the IP owner can no longer use that IP. A sole license also gives a single licensee rights to use the IP, however, the licensor retains the right to also use the IP. A non-exclusive license means that other people can also acquire a license to use that same IP.

Freedom to operate (FTO)

You must acquire an **IP portfolio** that gives you the **freedom to operate**. This may mean a combination of one or more patents protecting any technology you have invented as well as one or more licenses giving you the right to use technology others have invented and patented. You will not be able to attract private investment from angel investors or VC firms if you do not have freedom to operate.

This means that as part of your business plan and product development plan, you need to work out exactly how you will develop your technology, including what other technologies you will need to use, who owns them, whether the owners are willing to license those technologies to you and whether you can afford the license/s.

Trade secrets

If your invention is not patentable *i.e.* it is not new, useful and non-obvious, you can still protect it as a trade secret. Most software applications are protected in this way as it is very difficult to patent software in the US, UK and Europe. Trade secrets can be indefinite, unlike patents which only last 20 years. Also, there are no registration costs or official application for a trade secret. You can sue someone for using your trade secret information without your consent. However, to be able to sue, you must keep your trade secret information, such as software code or manufacturing process, secret through a combination of secure storage, restricted access and non-disclosure agreements.

Copyright

Copyright protects any intellectual property that is the expression of original ideas. This includes novels, songs, blog posts, white papers and academic papers. Copyright law grants authors the exclusive right to copy, sell, perform and display their work and any derivative works. If you publish an academic paper, the journal that publishes your article will often ask you to sign your copyright over to them.

Copyright automatically exists on all work that is not published under a creative commons license or other open sharing license. You can get added copyright protection for valuable work by registering it at one or more national copyright offices.

Trademarks

Any sign, design or expression can be registered as a trademark. This prevents others from using that property without your permission (which you can give in the form of a license). Before you can trademark a name or design, you must check trademark databases to make sure it has not already been trademarked. If the name or design is not trademarked, it is quick, easy and cheap to register a trademark but you must do it in each country where you want protection. Alternatively, you can submit a single international trademark application to the World

Intellectual Property Organization (WIPO) and get protection in up to 114 countries.

> *You can reduce your trademark application fees from around 1,600 Swiss francs to only 65 Swiss francs by filing in an office of one of WIPO's Least Developed Countries.*

How to pay for IP protection

IP protection is expensive. You must file a patent in each country in which you seek protection. These costs can quickly add up. In the US, professional patent searches cost $1,000 to 3,000. Attorney fees to have a patent professionally drafted can be $16,000 or more. If other companies infringe on your patents, it can cost hundreds of thousands of dollars of legal fees to enforce your patent rights.

In the UK, it costs £3,000 to £5,000 to have a patent application professionally drafted and £25,000 or more to file a suite of international patent applications. You also may have to pay £4,000 to £8,000 in additional costs to address any Patent Office objections.

These fees are all per patent. If you need multiple patents in multiple jurisdictions, how will pay for this?

If you invented your technology at a university or research institute, they will pay for the patent costs and then may enter into a licensing agreement with you, whereby they cover their patenting costs by retaining a small percentage of equity in the company you create and by keeping rights to a share of future profits. If the institution thinks the technology is very valuable, they will ask for higher percentages of equity and revenue sharing.

If you own your technology, then you are responsible for protecting it. If you cannot afford patent drafting fees, you can look for attorneys or law firms who are used to working with startups and are willing to defer their fees, up to a certain threshold, until an agreed date such as when you reach a funding milestone.

Further resources

Here are some free online resources where you can find more information about the concepts outlined in this chapter.

European Patent Office: https://www.epo.org/learning-events/materials/inventors-handbook/novelty/prior-art.html

European Union Intellectual Property Office Trademark Information: https://euipo.europa.eu/ohimportal/en

Patent Cooperation Treaty: http://www.wipo.int/pct/en/

UK Intellectual Property Office: https://www.gov.uk/government/organisations/intellectual-property-office

US Copyright Office: https://www.copyright.gov/

World International Property Organization (WIPO) international trademark system: http://www.wipo.int/madrid/en/

World International Property Organization (WIPO) Least Developed Countries: http://www.wipo.int/research/en/about/ldcs.html

USPTO Trademark Database: https://www.uspto.gov/trademarks-application-process/search-trademark-database

Chapter Three: Regulatory Compliance

Regulatory rules vary in different countries and you will need to check with each national regulatory body to ensure you are following the rules for that particular country. However, there are some standard guidelines and steps that many countries follow.

At the moment, the biggest biopharmaceutical markets in terms of potential revenue are the US and Europe. Therefore, I will give a brief overview of current regulatory pathways for drug candidates and medical devices in these two markets. These pathways do change from time to time as regulatory bodies introduce new regulations so it is important to regularly check in with national regulatory bodies and regulatory affairs professionals to make sure that you are following all necessary guidelines to have your products approved.

There is an excellent open access article that goes over this subject. The article is entitled "Drugs and Devices: Comparison of European and US Approval Processes" and was published in the Journal of the American College of Cardiology in August 2016.

While this chapter outlines some of the regulatory concerns faced by life science entrepreneurs, it does not offer regulatory compliance advice. Regulatory compliance is key to building a successful biotech company. Entrepreneurs can bootstrap and DIY many things, however, I highly recommend you seek professional help for regulatory compliance.

Regulatory basics

Here are some basic regulatory guidelines that you will need to follow regardless of where you are manufacturing and selling your products.

Good Manufacturing Practice

If you are manufacturing drugs or medical devices, you will need to abide by **Good Manufacturing Practice** (GMP), also called Quality System (QS) Regulation. GMP is a set of guidelines covering the production of drugs, devices or food for humans and is designed to ensure all approved products are safe for human use. The guidelines cover all aspects of production including the starting materials, premises, equipment, staff training and hygiene, and packing of the final product. It is essential that you document all procedures used at every step during production to prove that you have followed GMP. The exact documentation required will vary from country to country.

Good Clinical Practice

If you are running clinical trials with human subjects, whether the trials are for drugs, medical devices or clinical software, you will need to follow **Good Clinical Practice** (GCP). GCP is a set of international standards, both scientific and ethical, that outline how to design, record and report clinical trials on humans. These standards are based on the World Medical Association's Declaration of Helsinki which was first published in 1964, with the goal of protecting any humans who take part in clinical research. You can find a list of FDA regulations relating to GCP and clinical trials on the FDA website (listed in the 'Further Resources' section of this chapter).

ISO 13485

ISO 13485 is an international quality management system for medical devices. It has been drafted based on regulatory guidelines from many different countries. It outlines the quality management system requirements to produce medical devices that comply with regulatory requirements. The current version is ISO 13485:2016. If you apply for ISO 13485 certification, it can help with regulatory approval of your medical device in major markets around the world including the US, Europe and Canada. You can purchase the ISO 13845:2016 guidelines from the International Organization for Standardization website for 158 Swiss francs.

US drug and medical device regulations

In the US, all drugs and medical devices designed for human use must be approved by the Food and Drug Administration (FDA).

Any establishment that manufacturers, repacks or re-labels a drug in the US must register with the FDA.

Drug candidates

The FDA's Center for Drug Evaluation and Research (CDER) and Center for Biologics Evaluation and Research (CBER) are responsible for approving new drug applications. The CBER reviews all products derived from human or animal cells, gene therapy products, vaccines, allergenic extracts, antitoxins, antivenins and venoms, blood, blood components and plasma derived products. All other therapeutic products are regulated by the CDER.

Drug development in the US follows these steps:

- Preclinical studies
- Investigational New Drug Application
- Phase I Clinical Trials (Safety)
- Phase II Clinical Trials (Proof of Concept i.e. proof that your drug works to treat the chosen indication/s)
- Phase III Clinical Trials (Proof for Regulatory Approval)
- New Drug Application
- FDA Approval
- Phase IV Clinical Trials (Post-Marketing Safety Monitoring)

Once you have sufficient preclinical data, you must submit an **Investigational New Drug (IND)** application before conducting any clinical trials in humans. The FDA recommends taking part in the Pre-IND Consultation Program to receive guidance on the data you will need to submit an IND. INDs are either commercial or research and are further broken down into Investigator, Emergency Use or Treatment INDs. All IND applications must include animal pharmacology and toxicology data, any data in humans collected in foreign countries, manufacturing information, clinical trial design, clinical protocols and investigator information. Trial design should include whether or not the trial is randomized, controlled and blinded and if not, why not.

The FDA will send you an IND acknowledgement letter to let you know the date they received your IND. You can start clinical trials 30 days after the FDA received your IND, unless the FDA contacts you to say otherwise. You can find more information on IND applications on the FDA website.

The FDA monitors all clinical trials and conducts on-site inspections of clinical trials through its bioresearch monitoring (BIMO) program. The CDER or CBER can impose a clinical hold on a trial if there are safety concerns.

In all cases, you will need medical professionals to help run the trials. You can save a lot of time and money by employing a clinical trial consultant to design and run your trials and write your regulatory submissions.

Clinical trials for drug candidates in the US are conducted in four phases:

- Phase I (Safety): Researchers test the safety and side effects of an experimental drug in 20 to 100 healthy volunteers for the first time. This data helps to establish a safe dose range in humans and to understand the pharmacokinetics (absorption, distribution, metabolism and excretion) of the drug in humans.
- Phase II (Proof of Concept): Researchers further test the efficacy and safety of the experimental drug in up to several hundred people with a specific disease or condition. This data must show that the drug interacts with its target molecule and improves one or more clinically relevant outcomes in a patient population. Phase II trials also help to establish the best dose range and dosing regimen and to discover common side effects.
- Phase III (Evidence for Regulatory Approval): Researchers test the effectiveness, safety and side

effects of the experimental drug in 300 to 3,000 people and compare this data with placebo and/or with the standard of care for that disease.

- Phase IV (Post-Marketing Surveillance): The drug has now been approved by the FDA and marketed and Phase IV trials monitor drug safety and risks in several thousand volunteers. This may include trialing the drug in children or other new patient populations.

If you pass the safety requirements in Phase I-III clinical trials, you can submit all data collected from these trials, along with all your preclinical data and labeling information to the FDA in a **New Drug Application**. The FDA uses this information to decide whether the drug is safe and effective in its proposed use/s, whether the benefits outweigh the risks of using the drug, whether the proposed labeling and package insert are appropriate and whether the manufacturing processes are acceptable. NDA review includes a site visit by the CBER or CDER to evaluate your manufacturing processes and collect drug samples for analysis.

You can find forms and guidelines for NDA submissions on the FDA website. The exact requirements in an NDA depend on the nature and components of the drug candidate but may contain the following sections:

- Index
- Summary
- Chemistry
- Manufacturing and Controls
- Labeling
- Nonclinical Pharmacology and Toxicology
- Human Pharmacokinetics and Bioavailability

- Clinical Data
- Safety Report
- Statistics
- Case Reports
- Patent Information
- Patents

Once the FDA reviews an NDA, it will send you a letter stating that the drug is either: Not Approvable, Approvable or Approved. A Not Approvable letter will explain why the drug cannot be approved. An Approvable letter will explain any minor changes you need to make before the drug can be approved.

The FDA has an accelerated approval process for certain drugs. You can fast track FDA approval of drug candidates if they meet the requirements for **Fast Track**, **Breakthrough Therapy** or **Priority Review**.

The fast track process speeds up review of drugs that treat serious conditions or fill an unmet medical need such as Alzheimer's disease, heart failure or cancer. If you want to fast track your drug application and there are already drugs on the market to treat the same disease, you must show that your drug has superior effectiveness or patient outcomes or less side effects than current treatment options.

A drug is considered a Breakthrough Therapy if it treats a serious condition and your preliminary data shows the drug is substantially superior to current drugs in one or more clinically significant endpoints.

You can apply for Priority Review if you have evidence that your drug outperforms those on the market by being more effective, having fewer or less severe side effects or improving patient compliance. Priority Review cuts review time from ten months to six months.

If you are planning on selling generic drugs once the patents on a brand name drug have expired, you will need to submit an Abbreviated New Drug Application rather than an NDA. You will find it very difficult to get private investment to develop a generic drug.

Medical Devices

If you are developing or manufacturing a medical device in the US, the first regulatory step is to register your place of business as an 'establishment' with the FDA's Center for Devices and Radiological Health (CDRH). This is free and must be done within 30 days of producing a device or at least 90 days before you want to start selling your device.

You also need to list your device with the CDRH using their online form. This step is also free. You need to know which class your device belongs to at the time of listing.

Medical devices can vary widely in how invasive they are and what risks they pose to human health. The FDA classifies devices into Class I, Class II or Class III based on the risks inherent in the *intended use* and in the *indications for use* of the device. Class I devices carry the lowest risk and Class III have the highest. The different regulatory pathways for each class reflect this risk. You can find how to classify your device by looking in the FDA's classification database.

Class I devices have minimal potential to harm a user *e.g.* an elastic bandage. 95% of Class I devices are exempt from premarket submission, which means that you do not need FDA approval before marketing your device. However, for the other 5%, you will need to submit a **Premarket Notification**, also called a **510(k).** A 510(k) must show that your device is **substantially equivalent (SE)** to a device that is currently on the market and is *not subject to premarket approval.* To be substantially equivalent, a new device must have the same intended use and use the same sort of technology as an existing device. You must also show that your device is as safe as an equivalent device on the market.

Laboratory-Developed Tests

You can test a device without approval if it is considered a ***Laboratory-Developed Test*** *(LDT). An LDT is an in vitro diagnostic test that has been developed, manufactured and used within the same laboratory. If any of the development, manufacturing or use has been conducted outside of one laboratory, the test cannot be considered an LDT. LDTs do not currently need regulatory approval but the FDA is setting up new guidelines to cover this class of devices.*

Class II devices have some potential for harm *e.g.* an electric wheelchair. For most Class II devices, you must submit a Premarket Notification 510(k). In these cases, you must also abide by a number of rules including post-market surveillance and maintaining patient registries. For some Class II devices, you will need to submit a **Premarket Approval (PMA) Application** before you can market your device. Other Class II devices require no approval before going to market. The FDA website has a list of these Class II devices.

Class III devices are life-supporting or life-sustaining devices that prevent the impairment of human health. This includes devices such as surgical implants. A Premarket Approval (PMA) Application must be submitted for all Class III medical devices. The application must include all preclinical and clinical data. You will need to provide human clinical trial data. A regulatory expert can help you determine whether your device is likely to be a Class III device and what data you will need for approval. The FDA also offers formal collaboration meetings to help you decide whether or not you need human clinical trial data for approval.

When reviewing a PMA application, the FDA decides whether the device is safe and effective and whether it will 'significantly help a large portion of the target population'. You need to provide enough scientific evidence to show that each device is safe and effective. You cannot infer this from data about another device. The FDA calls this '**independence**'. The FDA will also inspect the premises where you manufactured your device. Your device will not be approved if these premises and all your manufacturing processes do not abide by Good Manufacturing Practice.

All Class III and some Class II medical devices require clinical trials to acquire the data needed for a PMA. Before conducting any clinical trials of a medical device in humans in the US, you must first request approval from the FDA's Center for Devices and Radiological Health. You can do this by applying for an Investigational Device Exemption (or less commonly for a Humanitarian Device Exemption).

An **Investigational Device Exemption** allows a new device to be used in a clinical study for the purpose of collecting data on the safety and effectiveness of the device. This exemption requires that any investigators receive hands-on training in how to use the device before starting the trial.

An IDE application should include the following sections:

- Background on the target disease, the study goals and how this study will further scientific knowledge
- Detailed description of the medical device

- Summary of any preclinical and clinical studies including safety data
- Explanation of whether preclinical studies have answered all safety questions
- Explanation of why a clinical trial is required
- Risk analysis including all potential risks to patients and a plan to mitigate those risks
- Plan for patient monitoring and follow-up
- Participant exclusion and inclusion criteria
- Sample size and number of investigational centers
- Informed consent document
- Primary and secondary endpoints: primary endpoints must be met for a trial to continue whereas secondary endpoints are desirable but not required
- Basic trial design – is it controlled, randomized, blinded? If not, why not?
- Data handling plan including case report forms. This ensures the right information is being collected to support your endpoints and that the data is being managed in compliance with HIPAA and HITECH regulations (more on this below)

A **Humanitarian Device Exemption** is available for devices designed to diagnose and/or treat orphan diseases (diseases or conditions that affect 4,000 or fewer patients each year in the US). This must be approved by the FDA before you can market your device.

Clinical trials for medical devices occur in three stages:

- Feasibility: preliminary safety and performance study in 10 to 30 patients with the target disease

- Pivotal: Efficacy and adverse effects study in 150 to 300 patients
- Post-approval: Long-term collection of safety, performance and side effect data

Feasibility and **Pivotal** trials need to be completed before you can submit a PMA. It may be unethical to design blinded medical device studies or studies with a placebo arm because, depending on the device, studies may involve invasive surgery e.g. if you are testing the safety and performance of a new surgical implant.

The FDA is reviewing their regulation of medical devices and of the newer sector of digital therapeutics. Therefore, regulatory rules and pathways are likely to change in the next few years.

Europe

Pharmaceutical drug and medical device development in Europe is regulated by the European medicines regulatory network, which comprises the European Medicines Agency (EMA), regulatory authorities in EU member states and in the European Economic Area, and the European Commission. It is more complicated than in the US as there is both centralized regulation by the EMA and decentralized regulation by EU member states. This regulation has been 'harmonized' so that each country follows the same standards and guidelines for approving drugs and medical devices.

Investigational medicinal products (drug candidates)

Medicines must be authorized before they can be marketed in Europe. You must submit a **Marketing Authorization**

Application (MAA) to the relevant regulatory authority. This can be done by a **centralized procedure**, where a single authorization application is submitted to the EMA or by a **decentralized procedure** where you simultaneously apply for authorization in multiple different countries. The rules and requirements are the same in both routes. You can also apply for authorization in one country and then apply for **mutual recognition** in all EU member states. Mutual recognition applications are submitted to the EMA.

The EMA is responsible for scientifically evaluating medicines. The EMA's scientific guidelines explain the specific rules that must be followed to have a new drug approved in Europe.

Clinical trials are authorized and monitored by the regulatory body or bodies of the EU countries in which the trials take place, not by the EMA. Clinical trials in Europe follow the same phases as those in the US: Phase I-III occur before marketing authorization. All clinical trials conducted in Europe must comply with the EU clinical trial legislation (Directive 2001/20/EC). This directive will be replaced with the new clinical trial Regulation EU 536/2014 in 2018.

The first step to conducting a clinical trial for an **investigational medicinal product** (IMP) in Europe is to register the trial on the European Clinical Trials (EudraCT) Database and obtain a EudraCT number. This database is maintained by the EMA. You also need approval from an ethics committee.

Then you must apply for a **Clinical Trial Authorization** (CTA) from the relevant regulatory authorities in each European country in which you wish to conduct the trial. You can submit clinical trials through the Common European Submission Portal (CESP), provided by the Heads of Medicines Agency (HMA). The CESP is a single platform that allows you to communicate with regulatory agencies across Europe.

If you wish to run a clinical trial only in the UK, you must submit a CTA to the Medicine and Healthcare products Regulatory Agency (MHRA). The MHRA recommends you contact them ahead of time and provide them with a preclinical data package if you are planning on conducting any **first-in-human** (FIH) studies with a novel compound.

A CTA application should include:

- A cover letter
- A clinical trial application form
- A clinical trial protocol
- An investigator's brochure
- An investigational medicinal product dossier (IMPD)
- A summary of any advice received from the EMA or any member state
- The EMA's decision on a pediatric investigation plan, if applicable
- A manufacturer's authorization on Good Manufacturing Practice for each site that will manufacture your investigational medicinal product (IMP)
- Labeling content for your IMP

Just as in the US, you can only proceed to the next phase of clinical trials if each trial meets minimum safety and efficacy requirements. These requirements must be explained in your application.

Once you have successfully completed Phase I-III clinical trials, you can apply for marketing authorization which will allow you to market your product in Europe. Marketing authorization follows these steps in Europe:

1. You submit an eligibility request
2. You submit a notification of intention to submit an application
3. The Committee for Medicine Products for Human Use (CHMP) (which is part of the EMA) appoints rapporteurs to conduct the scientific assessment of your drug
4. You have pre-submission meetings with the EMA
5. You submit your marketing authorization application
6. The CHMP performs scientific evaluation of your application
7. The CHMP issues a scientific opinion and sends this to the European Commission
8. The European Commission decides whether the new marketing authorization is approved

Like in the US, there are fast tracked application options for orphan drugs or emergency use of drugs in life-threatening situations.

Medical Devices

New European regulations on medical devices were issued on April 5, 2017, but will not come into force until 2020 for medical devices and 2022 for *in vitro* diagnostic devices. The new framework is called Medical Device Regulation.

The same medical device classes apply in Europe as in the US. Class I devices are low risk, Class IIa and IIb devices are medium risk and Class III devices are high risk.

Every medical device sold in Europe must have a Conformité Européenne (CE) mark showing that it complies with the essential requirements of European health, safety and environmental protection laws. This essentially means that the device works as you intend it to work and that any benefits outweigh any risks to patients. To receive a CE mark, you must follow these steps:

If you are a manufacturer outside of the European Economic Area, you will need to appoint a European Authorised Representative to help you liaise with European regulatory bodies.

1. Identify the EU requirements for your product. The Regulation (EU) 2017/745 now covers medical devices and the Regulation (EU) 2017/746 now covers *in vitro* diagnostics.
2. Check whether your product meets all legal requirements.
3. Check whether your product must be tested by a **Notified Body**. All Class II and III devices and any Class I devices that are sterile or have a measuring function must be tested.
4. Test your product for conformity to requirements. You must then draw up a Declaration of Conformity that includes the manufacturer's name and address, essential characteristics of the product, the identification number of any Notified Body and a legally binding signature.
5. Compile the technical dossier. This must contain enough information to prove that your product conforms with any regulatory requirements and will include a clinical evaluation report (CER).

A clinical evaluation report (CER) is required to comply with the MDR 2017/745 regulations and must be updated every one to five years even if your device has already received a CE mark. A CER should analyze clinical data to show that a medical device is clinically safe and performs as it should.

Notified bodies are independent companies designated by an EU member states to oversee testing of medical devices. There are more than 50 notified bodies and companies are free to choose any of them to test their devices.

As a manufacturer, it is your responsibility to choose a conformity route *i.e.* whether you want to show that your device confirms to EU standards by a combination of analyzing the literature to show that similar devices conform and doing preclinical testing in animal models or whether you will clinically test your device in humans. You can find out more about these options in the new regulations (EU) 2017/745 for medical devices and (EU) 2017/746 for *in vitro* diagnostics. You can also discuss this decision with your chosen notified body as they have a lot of experience doing this work and will know which is the better route in your specific circumstances.

Notified bodies may then conduct a full quality assurance by assessing your quality system and device design, testing all batches of your products and verifying the technical information in your technical dossier. They are also required to conduct unannounced audits of manufacturers.

Regulations on collecting and storing patient data

If you collect any patient data, such as contact details of anyone interested in news about your product development, you have to abide by **HIPAA** (Health Insurance Portability and Accountability Act of 1996) and **HITECH** (Health Information Technology for Economic and Clinical Health) regulations in the US and the **General Data Protection Regulation** (GDPR) in the EU. These regulations are designed to protect individual data privacy rights.

HIPAA

The Health Insurance Portability and Accountability Act of 1996 regulates the collection, storage, use and disclosure of Protected Health Information - all information about health, healthcare and healthcare payment. Therefore, if you choose to collect data, even names and email addresses, of patients, and this data includes their health status or anything about their health insurance or healthcare, you must store and use this data in accordance with HIPAA guidelines. Penalties for non-compliance are steep - up to $1.5 million for each breach.

Regulatory consultants or legal experts can help you design a checklist to ensure that you are meeting all guidelines. Here are some basic points that should be included in any checklist:

- An individual must give written permission to use their health information for marketing.
- All Protected Health Information must be encrypted and safely stored within a data center. There are a

number of online platforms that can provide this service. Make sure they are HIPAA and HITECH compliant before using them.

- All emails must be sent securely through a portal and patients should be given log in credentials to access emails so they cannot forward them to others.
- Anyone who has access to Protected Health Information should sign employee contracts or non-disclosure agreements preventing them from disclosing this information or using it outside of the scope of their work for your company.

Pryv is a data management platform that facilitates health data storage and transmission to guarantee regulatory compliance in jurisdictions around the world. They have developed tools for entrepreneurs who are creating products and services that handle personal medical and health information.

What is marketing?

Under HIPAA and HITECH regulations, the term 'marketing' means any communication that encourages someone to pay for a product or service. You must obtain written authorization from an individual before using their Protected Health Information for marketing purposes.

HITECH

The Health Information Technology for Economic and Clinical Health (HITECH) was passed in 2009 as part of the American Recovery and Reinvestment Act. HITECH regulates the use of health information technology such as electronic health records. The penalty for each violation is up to $1.5 million.

GDPR

The General Data Protection Regulation (GDPR) was approved in 2014 by the EU Parliament and will be enforced from May 2018. The GDPR aims to harmonize data privacy laws in European countries. It regulates data collection and use to sell goods or services to citizens of EU member countries. GDPR rules apply to all companies using the personal data of EU citizens, even if those companies are based outside of the EU. Penalties for breaches, such as not having customer consent to use their data, can be up to €20 million.

The GDPR defines 'personal data' as any data that could be used to identify an individual. This includes name, email address, photos, social media posts, computer IP address and medical data. Under GDPR, customers must give clear consent to use their data for marketing purposes. This means you must have easy-to-understand 'opt-in' and 'opt-out' options for all your marketing channels.

You can find the full GDPR on the official GDPR Portal website listed in the 'Further Resources' section of this chapter.

Further resources

Free online resources where you can find more information about the concepts outlined in this chapter.

Clinical trials for medical devices: FDA and the IDE process: http://www.cer-vd.ch/fileadmin/user_upload/documents/FL_FDAMD_20140815.pdf

Clinical trials – Regulation EU No 536/2014: https://ec.europa.eu/health/human-use/clinical-trials/regulation_en

Clinical trials for medicines: apply for authorization in the UK: https://www.gov.uk/guidance/clinical-trials-for-medicines-apply-for-authorisation-in-the-uk

Common European Submission Portal: https://cespportal.hma.eu/Account/CompanyRegistration

EudraCT European Clinical Trials Database: https://eudract.ema.europa.eu/eudract-web/index.faces

European Clinical Trial Legislation Directive 2001/20/EC: http://eur-lex.europa.eu/LexUriServ/LexUriServ.do?uri=OJ:L:2001:121:0034:0044:en:PDF

EU General Data Protection Regulation: http://www.eugdpr.org/

European Medicines Agency: Clinical trials in human medicines:
http://www.ema.europa.eu/ema/index.jsp?curl=pages/special_topics/general/general_content_000489.jsp

FDA Device Registration and Listing:
https://www.fda.gov/MedicalDevices/DeviceRegulationandGuidance/HowtoMarketYourDevice/RegistrationandListing/default.htm

FDA Medical Devices:
https://www.fda.gov/MedicalDevices/

FDA Registration and Listing:
https://www.fda.gov/forindustry/fdabasicsforindustry/ucm234625.htm

FDA Resources on Drugs and Devices:
https://clinicaltrials.gov/ct2/info/fdalinks

HIPAA for Professionals: https://www.hhs.gov/hipaa/for-professionals/index.html

HIPAA Marketing Guidelines from the US Department of Health & Human Services:
https://www.hhs.gov/hipaa/for-professionals/privacy/guidance/marketing/index.html

HITECH Act Enforcement Interim Final Rule:
https://www.hhs.gov/hipaa/for-professionals/special-topics/HITECH-act-enforcement-interim-final-rule/index.html

International Organization for Standardization ISO 13485:2016: https://www.iso.org/standard/59752.html

Chapter Four:
Plan Your Product Development

In this book, I use the term 'product development' to mean development of any application *i.e.* any product, platform or service. Life science entrepreneurs develop many different types of applications including: new drug candidates; medical devices; laboratory equipment and consumables and digital health management solutions. Each of these product types has different regulatory and reimbursement concerns, will follow different development timelines and will demand different pricing structure and sales and marketing strategies.

Investors will only invest in your company if you are developing an application with a good product/market fit.

When looking at your viable option list (the different applications you could develop from your intellectual property), it can help to sketch out a product development plan for each. This will help you to appreciate any difference in regulatory guidelines and reimbursement limits as well as how long it will take and how much it will cost to develop each different application. Once you have this knowledge, it should be easier to decide on which application to pursue first.

When outlining your product development plan, break it down into stages and milestones. Find out exactly what you need to do to get to each milestone and how long will it take. Work out how much it will cost. Where will that money, time and expertise come from? If you cannot do everything, who will help you? Where will you find those people? How will you compensate them—will they become co-founders, will you pay them in cash or offer equity or will they be partners?

Include your regulatory and reimbursement strategies in your product development plan. You cannot market a regulated product if it is not approved. Even if it is approved, if payers will not pay for it, you will find it very difficult to sell. Investors will want to see your regulatory and reimbursement plans.

Speak with other entrepreneurs and mentors to get an idea of how long each step will take, what data you need to proceed to the next stage and whether you will need to partner with other scientists or organizations to generate that data. Talk to people who have created similar applications and people who have developed completely different applications. Listen to their advice and learn from their mistakes.

Target Product Profile

The FDA recommends that life science companies use **Target Product Profiles** (TPPs) when developing therapeutics, medical devices and diagnostics. FDA review times are generally shorter for product candidates that have a TPP than for those that don't. A TPP outlines the ideal characteristics of your product, including how it compares with the current standard of care. If your product is not better than the current standard of care, it is unlikely to be approved. A TPP also lists the studies required to show that your product meets minimum safety and efficacy benchmarks.

You should include a **minimally acceptable product description** in your TPP. This outlines the minimum safety and efficacy benchmarks that your product must reach to continue development.

The FDA offers guidelines on how to write a TPP for life science products. This document is listed in the 'Further Resources' section at the end of this chapter.

A TPP can form the backbone of your product development plan. It is worth taking the time to write a TPP at the beginning of your product development cycle because it will focus your ideas and help you understand the best indication/s for your product and how you should develop your product to best meet those indications.

A TPP gives you the blueprint from which you can design your clinical trials. It gives you clear milestones in terms of safety and efficacy. If you do not meet those milestones at any stage of development, you will know that you have to go back and redesign your chemical compound or your delivery technology in the case of a therapeutic, or your hardware, software or reagents in the case of a device or diagnostic. While this decision is always painful, it saves a lot of time and money if you get there earlier rather than later.

If you are developing a non-clinical product, you could still write a TPP as it will help you reach go/no-go decisions sooner which will ultimately save you time and money and help you develop a better product.

Like your marketing plan and business plan, your TPP and product development plan should be a fluid document that you update as needed.

Drug Candidate TPP Template

This is an outline of how to write a TPP for a drug candidate. It can be used as a draft document from which you can write your product label if you advance to the stage where you can submit a new drug application (NDA) to the FDA or a marketing authorization application (MAA) to the EMA.

Product Description

Describe your product candidate and target molecule and give a brief overview of desired dose route and frequency.

Indication for use

Explain the unmet medical need that your drug candidate can treat. Describe your target patient population and outline how your drug will be administered to these patients - oral or injected? Capsule, tablet or sublingual wafer? Intravenous or subcutaneous injection? Who will administer the drug - the patients or a healthcare worker? Can it be taken at home or does it need to be administered in a clinic or hospital? Are any accompanying diagnostics required to monitor a patient's reaction to the drug?

Mechanism of Action

Explain which molecule your drug compound targets and how that will affect the molecular mechanism of disease pathogenesis.

Dosage and administration

Outline your target dose range, frequency and method of administration, including who will administer the drug and where. Include optimal (best case), target (most likely) and minimal accepted (worst case) dose ranges and routes.

Safety endpoints

List your preclinical and clinical safety endpoints. List your optimal, target and minimal accepted values for each endpoint. If you do not meet minimal accepted values for one or more endpoints, you need to discuss whether you should push forward in development or whether you need to redesign certain product features.

> ***Drug administration***
>
> *Investors are wary of drugs that are difficult to administer or require administration in a hospital or clinic, such as intravenous infusions. Always investigate other administration methods such as oral delivery or dermal patches. These methods increase patient compliance and lower the cost of drug delivery and so are more attractive to investors and more likely to be covered by payers.*

Efficacy endpoints

List your preclinical efficacy endpoints. List your primary clinical efficacy endpoints, which are the clinically relevant endpoints that you must meet for a clinical trial to be successful. List any secondary clinical endpoints, which are desired but not required endpoints in a clinical trial. Clinically relevant endpoints must be related to a clinical improvement in your target patient population in order to demonstrate the efficacy required for regulatory approval. Include optimal, target and minimal accepted values for each endpoint.

Preclinical studies

Summarize any completed preclinical studies and collected data in preclinical models. Outline any **pharmacokinetic** (absorption, distribution and duration of action), safety and efficacy data in animal models. List any outstanding studies required before you apply to start clinical trials by submitting an investigation new drug application (IND) in the US or a clinical trial authorization (CTA) in Europe. Include optimal, target and minimally acceptable safety and efficacy endpoints for any animal trials.

Clinical trials

Summarize any completed clinical study data, including pharmacokinetic, safety and efficacy data. Outline a complete clinical trial plan (Phase I-IV) including trial design. Clinical trial plans should include:

- number of participants
- whether participants are healthy or have a particular disease condition
- age range and sex of participants
- other inclusion and exclusion criteria
- clinically relevant trial endpoints with optimal, target and minimally acceptable values for each endpoint
- where each trial will take place
- who will perform each trial

All trials should be controlled and double blinded if possible, compare your treatment with placebo or current standard of care, and have enough participants to collect clinically relevant data.

Your trials should be designed to collect the following information:

- adequate pharmacokinetic data on the absorption, distribution and duration of action of your compound
- a safe dosing range
- side effect profile
- demonstrate efficacy in neutralizing the molecular target and treating the target disease

Contraindications and drug interactions

List any expected contraindications and drug interactions. Describe how these contraindications compare with those of competing treatments.

Storage and handling

Outline expected storage requirements such as light exposure, temperature and expected shelf life.

Packaging

Outline your planned packaging for this product.

> ***Product development plan***
>
> *Turn your TPP into a product development plan by adding your reimbursement plan, a budget (including where the money will come from e.g. investment or partnership), and a timeline.*

Medical device TPP template

This is a template TPP for medical devices including diagnostics.

Product Description

Add a description of your device or diagnostic including regulatory classification, an outline of the technology on which your device is based and how your device works. List any differentiating features and show how your device compares with competing products. Is it substantially equivalent to any existing device? (This will simplify the regulatory process but make it harder to market your product.) List ideal design features. Explain whether your device will be used alone or with other devices or treatments.

Indication for use

Explain the unmet medical need that your device can address. Describe your target patient population and outline how this population will use your device. Which part of the body will it target and how? Is it invasive or non-invasive? Who will use it and where—the patient or a healthcare worker, in the home or in a clinic or hospital?

Safety and efficacy endpoints

List the preclinical and clinical safety and efficacy endpoints that you need to fulfill any regulatory requirements (see Chapter Three for an overview of regulatory requirements in the US and Europe). Include optimal, target and minimal values for each endpoint.

Preclinical and non-clinical studies

Summarize any non-clinical and preclinical data. Outline your non-clinical product development studies. How will you meet the Good Manufacturing Practice (GMP) guidelines? Where will your device be manufactured? Does it need to be sterile? How will you maintain sterility?

Outline your preclinical studies including toxicology and efficacy endpoints in animal models. Include optimal, target and minimal values for each endpoint.

Clinical Studies

Summarize any completed clinical study data, including toxicology and efficacy data. Outline a complete clinical trial plan (Feasibility, Pivotal and Post-Approval) including trial design. Clinical trial plans should include:

- number of participants
- whether participants are healthy or have a particular disease condition
- age range and sex of participants
- other inclusion and exclusion criteria
- clinically relevant trial endpoints with optimal, target and minimally acceptable values for each endpoint
- where the trials will take place
- who will perform the trials

Clinical software

Clinical software may be considered a medical device. If it is, it will require the same regulatory compliance as other medical devices.

PhysioWizard® is a clinical software designed to help healthcare providers triage and provide treatment plans for back pain sufferers. It was developed by chartered physiotherapist, Kirsten Lord and had to be CE marked before it could be used by customers in Europe.

Contraindications

List any expected contraindications.

Minimum viable product

The Lean Startup movement advocates that companies create a **minimum viable product** as quickly as possible and test different versions on small groups of customers. That is much easier to do if you are creating a tech product rather than a biotech product. Pharmaceuticals and medical devices are tightly regulated and there are few loop holes in these rules. However, if you are developing a device or a research tool, you can develop an early prototype, and if you are developing a drug, you can do early proof-of-concept studies in cells or animal models. These results will form your minimum viable product when you begin looking for investment.

Reimbursement

Whether or not insurance companies or national healthcare systems (payers) will pay for a product is called **reimbursement**. Your reimbursement strategy is a critical part of any product development plan. It can be easy to overlook this at the early stages of product development. However, a business must bring in a revenue to be successful and all investors look for a return on their investment. To achieve this, you must either successfully market one or more products or services or your company must be acquired. If payers will not pay for your product or service, you cannot bring in revenue. Likewise, if all products in your pipeline are unlikely to be reimbursed, these assets are not valuable and you are less likely to be acquired.

Reimbursement strategy

Early on in your product development cycle, you should sketch out a reimbursement strategy. Here is a basic template:

- Step 1: Identify the payers in the countries in which you wish to sell you product or service. In the US, they are Medicare, Medicaid and private health insurance companies. In the UK, it is almost exclusively the National Health Service (NHS), which offers free universal healthcare to UK residents. Other European countries have a combination of private and public health payers and both national and local pricing systems.

- Step 2: Search for reimbursement codes to see what similar products have been reimbursed by whom and for how much. These codes tell you what information you need to give payers so they will pay for your product. The codes will also give you an idea of the reimbursement limit for your product, which is the maximum amount that a payer will pay for your product. If you want to price your product above the reimbursement code limit, you must be willing to justify why. For example, if you have a drug that only needs to be dosed once a week instead of once a day, then your product will offer significant cost savings to the payer and will increase patient compliance. In this case, you could negotiate with payers. You can either search for these codes yourself, on the Centers for Medicare and Medicaid Services (CMS) website, or hire reimbursement consultants or an agency to ensure that you are developing a product that is likely to be reimbursed.

- Step 3: If there is no code for similar products, start the process of creating a new code. In the US, this means contacting the American Medical Association, the CMS and any patient advocacy groups or medical societies that are likely to support development of your product or service. A new code can take one to three years to be issued so it is important to start this process early.

- Step 4: Show cost-effectiveness and clinical efficacy to payers. Payers make decisions about whether or not to cover a certain product or service based on the economic value provided by that product or service. Therefore, to increase the likelihood that your product will be covered, you need to demonstrate how it is superior to competing products or to the current standard of care. You also need to show how the price that you want to set for your product is good value. This means showing that the use of your product will improve long-term survival and quality of life and will also lower overall healthcare costs in your target patient population.

Reimbursement in the US

In the US, reimbursement is a discussion between the CMS, hospitals, healthcare providers and health insurance companies. It is a complicated landscape, which is why you can benefit from the help of a reimbursement consultant or agency.

Reimbursement amounts for pharmaceuticals and medical devices are set by the CMS and by private health insurers. Payers pay for an entire treatment or procedure. These interventions may or may not include drugs or medical devices. Reimbursement codes for these procedures are called Healthcare Common Procedure Coding System (HCPCS) codes. You can search for these codes on the CMS website. If you find an HCPCS code that includes a similar product, you know that your product category has been reimbursed before and hence your product is more likely to be covered.

The CMS, which comprises the public healthcare insurance systems Medicare and Medicaid, decides which drugs it will cover. That is called their **formulary**. Hospitals and clinics also decide which drugs to include in each of their covered procedures.

To successfully market a drug or a medical device, you need to have a plan to make sure that your product is covered by the CMS and private health insurance companies and is used in covered procedures in as many hospitals and clinics as possible.

Pricing and Reimbursement in the UK

The NHS provides free universal healthcare in the UK. It is the largest healthcare provider in the world. Therefore, any reimbursement strategy in the UK must focus on whether the NHS will cover your product or service. All new suppliers must apply to become part of the NHS Supply Chain.

The NHS uses two pricing schemes for branded drugs: The Pharmaceutical Pricing Regulation Scheme and the Statutory Scheme.

The Pharmaceutical Pricing Regulation Scheme (PPRS) controls the price that the NHS will pay for any licensed, branded, prescription medicines. It does not control the price of generic or over-the-counter medications. Companies can choose whether or not to be part of the PPRS. If they choose not to be part of the PPRS, the price of their drugs is set by the Statutory Scheme. In the Statutory Scheme, the Secretary of State sets a maximum price at which a new product can enter the market.

While the two drug pricing schemes are UK-wide, drug and medical device reimbursement schemes are different in each country that makes up the UK (England, Scotland, Wales and Northern Ireland).

Countries use health technology assessments (HTAs) to decide whether they will cover a new product and how much they will pay for that product. HTAs look at the long-term health and economic benefits that a new product can provide to the entire national healthcare system.

In England, the National Institute for Health and Clinical Excellence (NICE) conducts HTAs. NICE provides recommendations for the NHS use of new medicines and treatments. NICE appraisals are collated into Innovation Scorecards, which are published every three months on behalf of the Office for Life Sciences. NICE also provides access to the British National Formulary (BNF), an online reference database of drugs used in the UK.

HTAs are performed by the Scottish Medicines Consortium in Scotland, the All Wales Medicines Strategy Group in Wales and the Department of Health in Northern Ireland.

The Office for Life Sciences has a new online portal that provides information on all aspects of life science product development, including reimbursement strategies in the UK and the US.

Reimbursement in Europe

Under the Treaty on the Functioning of the European Union (TEFU), each EU member state is free to set its own pricing and reimbursement for life science products. Some countries set national reimbursement strategies and other countries set regional strategies. Reimbursement for new products in Europe is based on health technology assessments (HTAs) where the long-term economic and health benefits of any new technology are analyzed. This system is also called value-based pricing. There are around 100 HTA organizations across Europe. These organizations are overseen by the European Network for Health Technology Assessment.

Similar to the US, most European payers will pay for an entire medical intervention that may or may not include drugs and devices. Unlike in the US, where reimbursement limits are set by payers, in many European countries, pricing and price limits are set by hospitals.

In some cases, national healthcare systems and other payers will only cover a product in patients for whom the treatment is effective.

Further resources

Free online resources where you can find more information about the concepts outlined in this chapter.

Journal articles

Breder C, Wenny D and Tyndall A. What's the Regulatory Value of a Target Product Profile? Trends in Biotechnology. 2017: http://www.cell.com/trends/biotechnology/fulltext/S0167-7799(17)30035-5

Gold, M. Getting reimbursement for your product in the United States. Bioentrepreneur. 2003: http://www.nature.com/bioent/2003/030601/full/bioent738.html

Nusgart, M. HCPCS Coding: An Integral Part of Your Reimbursement Strategy. Advances in Wound Care. 2013. https://www.ncbi.nlm.nih.gov/pmc/articles/PMC3865619/

Online resources

All Wales Medicines Strategy Group in Wales: http://www.awmsg.org/

British National Formulary: https://bnf.nice.org.uk/

Centers for Medicare and Medicaid Services 2017 ASP Drug Pricing Files: https://www.cms.gov/Medicare/Medicare-Fee-for-

Service-Part-B-Drugs/McrPartBDrugAvgSalesPrice/2017ASPFiles.html

Centers for Medicare and Medicaid Services Medicare CPT/HCPCS Codes: https://www.cms.gov/Medicare/Health-Plans/MedicareAdvtgSpecRateStats/Risk-Adjustors-Items/CPT-HCPCS.html

Department of Health in Northern Ireland: https://www.health-ni.gov.uk/

FDA Guidance for Industry and Review Staff: Target Product Profile – A Strategic Development Process Tool: https://www.fda.gov/downloads/Drugs/GuidanceComplianceRegulatoryInformation/Guidances/ucm080593.pdf

How are Medical Devices Reimbursed in Europe (by Synergus AB): http://www.rspor.ru/mods/congress/stokg13/10.pdf

National Institute for Health and Care Excellence: https://www.nice.org.uk/

Office for Life Sciences: https://lifesciences.trade.gov.uk/

Selling to the NHS: http://knowledge.nic.nhs.uk/documentDetails.aspx?docId=10
Scottish Medicines Consortium: https://www.scottishmedicines.org.uk/

Treaty on the Functioning of the European Union: http://www.wipo.int/wipolex/en/details.jsp?id=7874

Chapter Five: Talk to Other Entrepreneurs

There is no substitute for speaking with people who have done what you are trying to do. Other entrepreneurs can help you at every step of building a business. They have experienced the same challenges in the same environment. You can learn from their mistakes, their stories and their tips. Best of all, successful entrepreneurs will have built up an extensive network of entrepreneurs, mentors and investors and they may be able to introduce you to the right people when you are looking to expand your team, fill your advisory board and Board of Directors, find mentors or attract investment.

But where do you find these other entrepreneurs?

If you are in an established biotech hub like Boston or San Diego in the US and Oxford or Cambridge in the UK, there are many networking events and member organizations for life science entrepreneurs.

However, if you live outside of these hubs, it can be more challenging to find people with life science startup experience.

How to find entrepreneurs

Here are some places you can look for entrepreneurs no matter where you live.

Your institution

If your university or institute has a technology transfer office, they will be able to tell you whether any of the faculty or alumni of the institute have entrepreneurial experience.

Your institution may also have an Office of Training or an Office of Postdoctoral Affairs which organizes seminars and workshops for graduate students and postdocs. You could contact these offices and ask for business or entrepreneurial training sessions. Invited speakers may be able to help you tap into the local entrepreneur community.

Other scientists in your research area

You could research other labs working in a similar research area to see if those scientists have any patents. Many universities will list their current patents available for licensing on their website. This can help you to work out who owns similar technology, but it doesn't tell you who are the entrepreneurs at that organization. You could contact the technology transfer office to find out.

You can also ask colleagues if they know any scientists who have or have previously had startup companies. Your colleagues may be able to give you a personal introduction to one or more scientist-entrepreneurs which will make them more likely to respond to your request for a meeting.

Local business schools

If you cannot find any scientist-entrepreneurs in your local area, you may need to cast your net wider and start looking for non-biotech entrepreneurs. These people may not have battled the challenges specific to the life science industry, such as IP protection, regulatory compliance and long product development cycles, but they will have a lot of business-specific knowledge that can help you such as how to create a website or a pitch deck for investors or how to write a business plan.

Local business schools are a great source of budding entrepreneurs and of entrepreneurial faculty.

Entrepreneur organizations

Your town or city, or a nearby town, may have an entrepreneur organization with meetings that you could attend. If it isn't life science-specific, you could still learn a lot of tips and tricks by talking to local business people. If your local area has an Economic Development Office, they might be able to help put you in touch with local entrepreneurs.

> ***If at first you don't succeed...***
>
> *Entrepreneurs are busy. Professors are busy. These people will often not respond to your first email or social media request. This doesn't always mean that they will not respond to a second or third email. Be persistent but polite with your requests. Do not simply ask for help but offer something in return such as a collaboration opportunity. Become comfortable speaking about your technology without revealing confidential information. If you need to disclose confidential information, ask people to sign an NDA first.*

Entrepreneur platforms

There are a number of online communities for entrepreneurs. The online world is fickle, so the most active communities change over time but a couple of the bigger ones are a safe bet to start.

AngelList

AngelList is a community of startup entrepreneurs, freelancers and investors. The website has directories of startup companies, incubators and accelerators, and consultants looking for work. You can use AngelList to search for startups and apply for jobs in thousands of different startup companies. Or, if you have a startup, you can use the platform to look for employees, contractors or investors. Investors on AngelList include angels, VCs, family offices, institutions and accredited investors.

Crunchbase

Crunchbase is a database of companies, entrepreneurs and investors. It has reams of data on startup funding and investment and has hundreds of thousands of individual and company profiles. However, to access all that data, you need to pay a monthly subscription.

Life Science Network

Life Science Network is an online community of life science professionals including scientists, entrepreneurs and investors. It is free to join and members can search for other members with a particular job title or in a geographical area. Members can also post questions in discussion forums and access interviews with startup entrepreneurs.

Startup Grind

Startup Grind is a global entrepreneur community with in-person educational events for entrepreneurs. They have over 1,000,000 members in over 200 cities. They also run the Startup Program Global, which trains entrepreneurs on how to pitch, connects them to investors and showcases startups from around the world at the annual Global Conference Startup Showcase.

Social media

Social media is a good way to find people with various interests and a lot of people are more likely to respond to social media requests than to emails.

Social media platforms come and go and it can be overwhelming deciding which ones to join. It can also feel like a waste of time building a presence on several different platforms. However, social media is a powerful communication tool and it will help you build your network and start building your personal brand and the brand of your company (more on this in Chapter Twelve).

Where to start? Twitter, Facebook and LinkedIn are a good place to start. They've been around for a long time, in social media life span, and are likely to be here for a while longer. Facebook and LinkedIn both have thousands of entrepreneur and biotech groups and Twitter has a number of regular entrepreneur conversations which you can follow using hashtags (start with #entrepreneur and #biotech and see where the rabbit hole takes you).

Meetups

Entrepreneurs all over the world use Meetup to organize meetings and in-person events. You do not have to pay to join Meetup and search for meetings but you do have to pay if you want to organize a meetup through the website.

Co-working spaces

Co-working spaces are springing up across the world. Visiting a co-working space can help you meet local entrepreneurs in your area. These spaces also give you an affordable option if you are in need of office space or need a physical address for grant applications.

Community labs

The DIY hackerspace and community lab movement is growing around the world. These spaces offer shared lab space and equipment at very affordable prices to anyone who wants to join. Many community labs also offer educational events that are open to the local community, usually for a fee. More on community labs in Chapter Nine.

Incubators and accelerators

There are thousands of startup incubators and accelerators catering to various types of companies. Life science-specific incubators and accelerators offer wet lab space as well as office space. These are another excellent place to find entrepreneurs. Many incubators and accelerators also offer educational and networking events and workshops for their tenants. Some of these may be open to non-tenants. Do your research before signing up to join an incubator or accelerator as many will take equity in return for the use of their space and resources. More on incubators and accelerators in Chapter Ten.

Ad on Craigslist or Gumtree

If you can't find the right people to speak with, you could always put an ad up on Craigslist or Gumtree or the equivalent website in your country asking for help from local entrepreneurs.

Further resources

Free online resources where you can find more information about the concepts outlined in this chapter.

AngelList: https://angel.co

Craigslist: https://www.craigslist.org

Crunchbase: https://www.crunchbase.com/

Life Science Network:
http://lifesciencenetwork.com/home

Meetup: https://www.meetup.com/

Startup Grind: https://www.startupgrind.com/

Chapter Six: Choose the Right Co-founders

Starting a life science company is a mammoth task, especially if you are a first-time entrepreneur. One or more co-founders can help you 'divide and conquer' to tackle the never-ending list of tasks required to build a successful company.

The right co-founder can also help you to secure investment. When investors are deciding whether or not to invest in a company, one of the first things they look for is a well-rounded team that has previous startup experience. If you don't have any business experience, you can boost your chances of success by choosing a co-founder who does.

How many co-founders do you need?

In the book 'The Founder's Dilemmas', Noam Wasserman analyses data he collected from thousands of American high-tech and life science startups over a ten-year period from 2000 to 2009. He found that less than 12% of life science startups have a sole founder. The majority (over 65%) have either two or three co-founders. This makes sense as the major tasks required to build a life science company can be divided into science-based and business-based tasks.

Investors are wary of sole founder companies. They will often ask why you haven't managed to convince at least one other person to join you. Be prepared to defend that choice if you choose to be a solo founder.

Solo founders are responsible for managing all facets of their nascent company and can only tap into their own network for help. It takes a lot of time and energy to create extensive professional networks based on strong relationships. If you are a first-time entrepreneur, you are unlikely to know many investors or legal, regulatory or manufacturing specialists.

Bringing on one or more co-founders will help you expand the company's available skill set, expertise and network. It will also make the long and very bumpy road of life science entrepreneurship less lonely. And you may need someone to help you finance your company out of their own pocket before you attract private investment.

The downside to having co-founders is that you will have to share decision-making and equity. While this means that you may end up making better decisions for your company, because you have several view-points contributing to the decision-making process, it also means that it will likely take you longer to come to a consensus and you may have to relinquish some control of how your company will run. You will also own less of your company. However, bringing on co-founder/s may make your company more valuable. Until you take in revenue or sell your shares or your entire company, you will not see any financial reward. Your company is in some ways worthless. Entrepreneurs are fond of saying 100% of zero is zero.

What makes someone the right co-founder?

I ask every startup entrepreneur that I interview how they chose their co-founders. The most common answer is: someone with complementary skills. Entrepreneurs consistently cite 'complementary skills' as one of the biggest factors to consider when choosing co-founders, early employees and board members.

> *"Companies are all about the people and not about the technology. You may or may not need the technology to make your company work but if, as a CEO, you're not spending an awful lot of your time making sure people are happy and doing their job properly, it won't work."*
>
> ***Will Dracup, CEO and co-founder of Biosignatures***

Entrepreneurs are also quick to point out that being a startup co-founder is like being married. You will be working 100-plus hour weeks with this person (or people), often in cramped or shared work spaces because you have limited funding. You will face high levels of stress as you work to convince the world that your ideas, your science and your products are new, exciting and worthy of investment or purchase.

Will Dracup, a serial bioentrepreneur, believes that people can make or break a startup company. Will founded Nonlinear Dynamics, a proteomics software company in 1989 and sold it to Waters Inc. in 2013. Will was a sole founder at Nonlinear, but he chose to work with a co-founder when he spun-out his third company, Biosignatures.

When I spoke with Will about his startup journey, he cautioned that you need to choose a co-founder with whom you can work under pressure. “If the founders can’t get along, the whole thing will likely die,” he said.

Noam Wasserman’s data from ‘The Founder’s Dilemmas’ shows that startups are more likely to be successful if co-founders are either past colleagues or strangers than if they are friends or family.

Where to find the right co-founder?

Since so much is riding on finding the right co-founder/s, it can seem like a daunting task. You can use all the suggestions in the previous chapter of where to find entrepreneurs to also find potential co-founders. You can also tap into your network, both in the real world and online, by asking people if they know anyone with the particular skill set you need. Or attend one of the many large events that aim to help entrepreneurs meet each other, such as Startup Weekend or Startup Grind.

There are a number of websites that aim to cross-match co-founders or entrepreneurs. One of them is AngelList which I mentioned in the previous chapter. There is also FoundersNation. Another is CoFounders Lab, which has both an online matchmaking platform for entrepreneurs and real world networking events.

Before looking for a co-founder, you need to be clear about what you want in that person. Exactly what skills does that person need? What sort of experience? And what personal attributes? What sort of person could you get along with when working in a high-pressure environment?

Also, it helps at this stage to think about roles. Do you want to be CEO? If so, what role do you want your co-founder to have? What tasks and responsibilities will that role entail? If you have this ‘blueprint’ of the right person in your mind, it will be easier to find that person.

Part of searching for the right co-founder is being honest with yourself about your own skills, strengths, experience and personality. If you are aware of your deficits, you can search for someone who can plug these holes.

Even if you have known someone for years and know you can work very well together, don't choose that person if they have the same skills, experience and network as you. Ultimately that person will not help your startup succeed.

Equity Split

If you have co-founders, you will need to share equity equitably to keep everyone happy and to incentivize each person to keep advancing your product development and business plans. During the early days before you have secured funding, you may also choose to use equity instead of or as well as cash payment for early employees, contractors and board members.

Deciding how to split equity can be a very contentious issue. Everyone wants to maximize his or her gains so you will naturally have opposing views on who should receive how much. 'The Founder's Dilemmas' by Noam Wasserman and 'Slicing Pie' by Mike Moyer are two excellent books that describe methods for deciding on equity splits.

In an effort to keep your decision fair, you need to take in to account how much each person has already contributed to the company in terms of intellectual property, time, money and non-cash assets like equipment and facilities, as well as what they are likely to contribute in the future. Future contributions are much harder to predict and are likely to change over time. You also need to factor in the cost of any lost opportunities *i.e.* how much each of you could be earning if you weren't working on the startup.

Therefore, instead of choosing a permanent equity split early in your startup journey, it might work better to lay out a dynamic plan in which the split can change up to a predetermined amount depending on future contributions. Or you could set aside a pool of equity to be divided up based on future contributions.

It is also a good idea to choose to vest your equity over time or when milestones are reached. This means that you will only accrue your full amount of equity once a certain time has passed (*e.g.* four years) or once you have achieved certain milestones. This gives you a certain 'insurance' against co-founders leaving the company and taking a big chunk of equity with them. Many investors will require that founders' stock is vested. It will help if you have done this from the beginning. Then you won't have to 'lose' any of your stock when you attract private investment.

A common vesting schedule is four years with a one year cliff. This means that founders receive no stock for the first year, then receive 25% of their shares at the one year mark, and receive 1/48th of their shares every month thereafter. This means that all shares will be vested (received) after four years.

You should discuss what will happen with any vested and unvested (unallocated or unearned) equity if one or more co-founders choose or are forced to leave the company. You may want to include a mandatory buy-back clause in your founders' agreement that allows remaining founders or the company to buy vested shares at a predetermined price from any of the founders who leave. You might have different terms depending on whether someone chooses to leave, is forced out by other co-founders or the board, or has to leave for medical reasons.

Lastly, remember that your equity will be diluted with each funding round, except in the case of **non-dilutive**

funding such as government grants or loans. Non-dilutive funding does not require ownership of shares in your company in exchange for cash. This is in contrast to Angel or VC funding which offers cash in exchange for equity. Equity is generally divided into company shares.

As an example, before you receive any funding, you may have arbitrarily divided your company into 10 million shares. If you own 50% of the company, you own 5 million shares. An investor may give your company a pre-money valuation of $2 million. This is the estimated value of your company based on your IP, your team and any milestones you have achieved. In this example, the share price is $2 million/10 million shares = 20 cents. The investor may offer to invest $500,000 at that share price, which means you have to issue 2.5 million new shares. Now there is a total of 12.5 million shares. You still own only 5 million of those shares, so now you own 40% not 50% of the company. Your share has been diluted by the funding.

Difference between an advisory board and a Board of Directors

A startup looking for investment typically needs two different boards: an advisory board and a Board of Directors.

The **advisory board** is a group of domain experts who help you make business and scientific decisions for your company. If you want to attract well-respected and well-known people with a lot of experience, you may have to offer them a small amount of equity in exchange for joining your advisory board. This is not always required.

Set contracts for advisory board members that specify the duration of their role. This gives you an easy way to remove any advisors who are not contributing to your company. Advisors who are not involved can be a liability. If investors contact them and they don't know anything about your company, it reflects poorly on your company.

The **Board of Directors**, on the other hand, are legally liable for the actions of the company and have voting rights in any important company decisions. Most VCs take a seat on the Board of Directors of the companies in which they invest.

Alternatives to co-founders

There are alternatives to bringing on co-founders. You could develop a comprehensive business and product development plan where you **outsource** work to different experts. An extreme version of this is running a **virtual company**, where a core team essentially project manages a company and outsources all work to different contractors, contract research organizations and consultants.

Further resources

Here are the details of two excellent books that give you more information about the concepts outlined in this chapter.

'The Founder's Dilemma: Anticipating and Avoiding the Pitfalls That Can Sink a Startup' by Noam Wasserman: https://www.amazon.com/Founders-Dilemmas-Anticipating-Foundation-Entrepreneurship/dp/0691158304

'Slicing Pie: Funding Your Company Without Funds' by Mike Moyer: https://www.amazon.com/Slicing-Pie-Funding-Company-Without/dp/0615700624

Chapter Seven: Apply for Commercialization Grants

One of the recurring themes that comes through when I interview entrepreneurs is the advice to use government grants to fund your early-stage company. There are two very good reasons to do this. The first is that government grants are non-dilutive funding. That means that you do not have to give the granting agency any equity in your company in exchange for the funding. You also do not have to cede any control to investors. The second reason is that grant applications are reviewed by experts in your particular scientific field. If your grant application is funded, you have received external validation that your idea is worth funding. This is very valuable when it is time to convince investors to put their money into your company.

Bradley Messmer invented a novel technology to bind antibodies while he was a scientist at the University of California, San Diego (UCSD). He licensed this tech from UCSD and used it to spin out his company, Abreos Biosciences. Abreos is now developing tests that allow physicians to monitor antibody drug levels in patients' blood in real time. Messmer used six government grants as an early funding source.

> *"Grants give you credibility and show an investor that the science is real. Most angels don't have the ability to do deep due diligence in every area in which they might want to invest. So, it helps if you have the NIH stamp of approval."*
>
> ***Bradley Messmer, former academic scientist now CEO, Abreos Biosciences***

nanoComposix is another company built on grants. They chemically alter nanoparticles to create different optical effects. Their nanoparticles are used by partner companies and clients for a number of applications. nanoComposix has chosen to stay as a small company, with 35 employees, and to raise money through grants and corporate partnerships, rather than give up equity in exchange for private funding.

The major problem with government grants, is they run on a slow, academic-style time line. It can take six to nine months or longer to receive feedback on your application, and may take even longer to receive funding if you are successful. Also, any government-funded research must follow strict guidelines, such as ethics regulations on animal and human experiments. These are different from country-to-country and even from state-to-state.

Tips for Grant Applications

As all scientists know, grant writing is an art. Applying for commercialization grants is no exception. Just like with co-founders, when I ask life science entrepreneurs about grant writing tips, they often have similar answers. Tell a story and clearly present your data, experimental plan and milestones. Most of the time, the criteria for a commercialization grant are very similar to that of any private investor: Can **your team** create **a product** that fills a **large market need**?

Read successful applications

You can learn from other people's mistakes by reading successful (and unsuccessful) grant applications and working out where the differences are. Reading grant applications will also help you learn the sort of language that you need to use, the best layout to choose, as well as how you should present your data and argue your case. Ask colleagues if they know anyone who has had a commercialization grant funded and then ask that person if you could either read their application or if they have any tips they could share with you.

Plan early

You need to have enough data to convince reviewers to fund your grant application. You also need enough time to write the grant and you need enough funds to keep you going while you wait the six to nine-month lag time before you receive any grant money.

> *"Make sure you talk to the program officer and check that you are meeting their requirements. Get somebody else to read (your grant application) to make sure that it is easy to understand. Start planning and writing early."*
>
> ***Richard Baldwin, Chief Scientist of nanoComposix***

Know your audience

Different agencies have different agendas and different funding mandates. Apply to an agency that has a track record of funding technologies that are similar to your technology. Granting agencies will often have a program or grants officer whom you can contact with any questions you might have.

Commercialization grants are often reviewed by a mix of academics and industry professionals. They may not know your specific disease or area of research so explain your science in simple, clear terms that any intelligent person could understand.

Have a clear message

A grant application is similar to an investor pitch. You need to clearly articulate the problem you are addressing, explain your solution and outline why you are better than any competitors.

Jennifer Schneider is a Principal at Tiber Creek Partners, a consulting agency that writes grants for companies and academic scientists. "Show how what you are doing is really special – do you have a different way of thinking about the problem? How is your solution different?" Jennifer said. "We often leave a lot of interpretation to reviewers about the data or about the message. Make sure you say that this is special for these reasons. Here are these figures and this is what you need to know about them."

Address the review criteria

Review criteria will vary for each specific grant. Before you start an application, try to speak with grant officers from each granting agency to find out what review criteria they use. Make sure your application answers the fundamental question: Can **your team** create **a product** that fills a **large market need**?

For SBIR and STTR grants in the US, the review criteria are broken down into five sections:

1. Significance:
    - Does the project have the potential to lead to a marketable product?
    - Does the project address an important problem?
    - If this project is successfully completed, how will that change current methods, treatments and technologies in this field?
2. Investigators:
    - Are the investigators well-suited to the project?
    - Do investigators have appropriate experience and training?
3. Innovation
    - Does the application shift current research or clinical practice?
4. Approach:
    - Are the strategy and proposed methodology well-reasoned and appropriate?
5. Environment:
    - Does the team have enough institutional support or the necessary facilities and equipment to conduct the proposed experiments?

Explain your technology

Explain the background science. Explain your proposed application and how it is better than existing diagnosis or treatment methods. Generate enthusiasm. Have a defined product goal and a clear experimental plan. It doesn't matter how strong your science and your team are if your technology will not significantly change how a disease is diagnosed or treated or how experiments are currently performed.

Have specific milestones

Lay out specific scientific milestones and show how the grant funding will help you achieve these milestones sooner. Reviewers want to see that you need the grant money to achieve your milestones.

Show your IP protection strategy

Explain how you will protect your IP and prevent others from developing similar, and therefore, competing products.

Highlight your team and facilities

Outline the strengths and experience of your team. Reviewers need to see that you have people capable of performing your planned experiments and you have access to the resources and facilities required to conduct the experiments.

Include letters of support

Letters of support from any collaborators or potential customers can really help convince reviewers to fund your grant. Reviewers want to know that the product you are developing will solve a real-world problem. If you are developing a drug or medical device, try to get letters from physicians saying they would use your product and/or from patient advocacy groups explaining the importance of your solution.

Obey guidelines

Obey guidelines on where the company must be based and how much time each investigator devotes to the project, as well as animal and human welfare rules. If you say that the principal investigator has a full-time academic position, reviewers will probably not fund your application. They want to see that you have enough time to spend on your project.

Get feedback before submitting

Ask colleagues to read your application and give feedback. What didn't they understand? Did it excite them? Do they think this addresses a big market need?

Keep trying

If you don't succeed, take all reviewer feedback on board and try again. Many of the entrepreneurs I have spoken with have succeeded on their second or third try.

Where to find more tips

The NIH has a list of grant writing tips. If you are at a university or research institute, they may also have grant writing workshops or resources they can share with you.

US Commercialization Grants

In the US, commercialization grants are available at the federal, state and local level and also through private foundations.

Federal Grants

US federal agencies with R&D budgets of $100 million or more must spend a small portion of their budget (3.2% in financial year 2017) on grants that fund small businesses. To be eligible for these grants, small businesses must be doing research that could be commercialized.

The largest of these federal grant programs are the Small Business Innovation Research (SBIR) Program and the Small Business Technology Transfer (STTR) Program. Both these programs have the goal of stimulating technological innovation.

SBIR Program

Currently 12 federal agencies participate in the SBIR grant program. You can find a full list at: www.sbir.gov. Each agency chooses its own grant deadlines and will put out solicitations for grant applications. Each solicitation is for a specific topic or application. They change regularly and can be quite specific *e.g.* 'Nasal Delivery of CNS Therapeutics'.

SBIRs are divided into Phase I and II. Phase I funding is capped at $150,000 over six months and must be used to establish the feasibility and commercial potential of promising technology. If you receive a Phase I SBIR and you successfully achieve all the milestones laid out in your application, you can apply for a Phase II grant to continue your product development. Phase II awards are up to $1,000,000 in funding over two years.

STTR Program

The STTR Program promotes academic-industry collaboration. To be eligible for a Phase I or II STTR grant, a small business must partner with a research institution.

Otherwise, the program runs similarly to the SBIR program. Phase I STTR grants provide up to $150,000 for one year to show the feasibility and commercial potential of a technology. Phase II STTR grants are up to $1,000,000 for two years to extend this research.

NIH Commercialization Accelerator Program

The NIH Commercialization Accelerator Program (CAP) offers marketing, business strategy, regulatory and reimbursement support for companies that have received SBIR or STTR grants within the past five years.

Department of Energy Technology Commercialization Fund

The Department of Energy (DOE) launched the Technology Commercialization Fund in 2016. Companies developing novel technology in a number of energy sectors can apply for part of an annual pool of $20 million. However, any DOE funding must be matched by private funding sources.

State Grants

Many states across the US also have various grants and initiatives to support life science entrepreneurship. These are available through both public and private organizations. Here are a few examples:

- Massachusetts Technology Transfer Center
- Michigan Initiative for Innovation and Entrepreneurship
- New Jersey Commission on Science & Technology Grants & Initiatives
- New York State Empire State Development
- North Carolina Biotechnology Center

Other Grant Sources

You may also be able to find grants from Patient Advocacy Groups and Foundations, Gap Funding Programs at universities, local and state Offices of Economic Development, and Innovation Prizes offered by both government organizations and for-profit companies.

Europe

There are a number of Europe-wide initiatives to offer financial support and mentorship to science and technology startups.

Horizon 2020

The Horizon 2020 program will use €80 billion over seven years, from 2014 to 2020 to commercialize breakthrough technologies. The program's goal is to achieve sustainable economic growth for the EU. It is the financial part of the Innovation Union, an initiative to make the EU more research and innovation-friendly. Horizon 2020 comprises many different funding programs, all with their own eligibility requirements. For many of the programs, you will need to partner with at least one other organization to be eligible.

European Research Council Proof of Concept Grant

The European Research Council (ERC) is part of Horizon 2020. The ERC Proof of Concept Grants offer up to €150,000 for 18 months. The money may be used to set up a company, protect intellectual property and establish the viability of a nascent technology. This grant is only open to recipients of an ERC frontier research grant and principal investigators must be working at a research organization in the EU.

SME Instrument

The SME Instrument is another part of Horizon 2020, with €3 billion to fund small and medium-sized enterprises that are commercializing new technologies. The program is divided into three phases. Phase 1 offers up to €50,000 over six months for feasibility studies. Phase 2 offers €500,000 to €2.5 million over two years for prototype development, testing and scaling. Phase 3 offers coaching services and support through the Enterprise Europe Network. The program also offers free business coaching.

European Structural and Investment Funds

The European Structural and Investment Funds (ESIF) have a €110 billion purse to support innovation and small and medium-sized enterprises, including those developing bio-based products. Specific funding opportunities are listed on the European Commission website.

European Fund for Strategic Investment

The European Fund for Strategic Investment plans to raise €315 billion in funds to support investment across a range of areas including research and innovation. The fund is managed by the European Investment Bank. You can use an online tool, the European Investment Advisory Hub, to look for specific funding opportunities, both grants and loans, and other support such as expert advice and mentorship. You can also list your company on the

European Investment Project Portal and find potential investors.

Loans

If you are not eligible for grants, you may be eligible for a business loan, either through your bank or through a federal (national) or state program. While you will have to pay back a loan, plus any interest, you do not have to give up equity for this type of financing. Just as you would have to convince any potential investors of the viability of your company, you will have to prove to a bank that you are financially able to pay back a loan.

US Federal loans

A number of federal agencies including the Department of Energy and the National Oceanic and Atmospheric Administration (NOAA) offer loans and fund-matching programs. There are links to more information about these programs in the 'Further Resources' section at the end of this chapter.

US State loans

Many states also offer loans to support startups and small businesses. Here are a few examples:

- California Small Business Loan Guarantee Program
- Massachusetts Life Science Center Accelerator Loan Program
- New Orleans Biofund
- North Carolina Biotechnology Center Business Loans

European loans

Europe has several programs to help startups and small businesses secure loans.

InnovFin Program

The InnovFin Program is part of Horizon 2020 and is managed by the European Investment Bank Group. The program aims to invest €48 billion in research and innovation and offer €24 billion of loans and equity financing by 2020.

COSME

The Competitiveness of Small and Medium-Sized Enterprises (COSME) program has a budget of €2.3 billion to provide entrepreneurship education and mentoring to SMEs as well as facilitate access to financing through local banks in EU countries.

InfoRegio

The European Commission's InfoRegio site has information about other EU funding opportunities.

Further resources

Free online resources where you can find more information about the concepts outlined in this chapter.

Competitiveness of Small and Medium-Sized Enterprises (COSME) program:
http://ec.europa.eu/growth/smes/cosme/

Department of Energy Funding Opportunities:
https://energy.gov/energy-economy/funding-financing
Department of Energy Technology Commercialization Fund:
https://energy.gov/technologytransitions/technology-commercialization-fund

European Fund for Strategic Investment:
http://www.eib.org/efsi/

European Research Council Proof of Concept Grant:
https://erc.europa.eu/funding/proof-concept

European Structural and Investment Funds (ESIF) calls for proposals: https://ec.europa.eu/growth/contracts-grants/calls-for-proposals_en

Horizon2020:
https://ec.europa.eu/programmes/horizon2020/en/background-material

InfoRegio:
http://ec.europa.eu/regional_policy/index.cfm/en/funding/accessing-funds/

InnovFin – EU Finance for Innovators:
http://www.eib.org/products/blending/innovfin/index.htm

Massachusetts Life Science Center Accelerator Loan Program:
http://www.masslifesciences.com/programs/accelerator/

Massachusetts Technology Transfer Center:
http://www.mttc.org/about-mattcenter/overview/

Michigan Initiative for Innovation and Entrepreneurship:
https://www.masu.org/aboutmasu/partnerships/miie/

National Oceanic and Atmospheric Administration (NOAA) Funding Opportunities:
http://www.nmfs.noaa.gov/aquaculture/funding/funding.html

New Jersey Commission on Science & Technology Grants & Initiatives: http://www.state.nj.us/scitech/programs/

New Orleans Biofund:
http://www.neworleansbio.com/programs/biofund/

New York State Empire State Development:
https://esd.ny.gov/nystar/

NIH Commercialization Accelerator Program (CAP):
https://sbir.nih.gov/cap
NIH Grant Writing Tips:
https://grants.nih.gov/grants/grant_tips.htm

North Carolina Biotechnology Center:
http://www.ncbiotech.org/research-grants/research-funding

North Carolina Biotechnology Center Business Loans:
http://www.ncbiotech.org/growth

Small Business Innovation Research (SBIR) and Small Business Technology Transfer (STTR) Overview:
https://www.sbir.gov/about

SME Instrument:
http://ec.europa.eu/programmes/horizon2020/en/h2020-section/sme-instrument

Chapter Eight: Enter Startup Competitions

Startup competitions are about more than the chance to win funding or lab space. They also give you valuable opportunities to network, start building relationships, find mentors and learn from industry experts. The best competitions offer workshops that train participants on business basics like writing a business plan, creating a pitch deck and pitching to investors.

Talking to entrepreneurs and mentors can help you hone your product development and business plans and decide whether your startup idea is viable and your market assessment is accurate. Before speaking to anyone about your technology, you need to work out how to talk about it without compromising your IP protection. This means learning how to accurately describe your basic concepts without sharing specific proprietary or confidential details.

> *"I had a lot of help from advisors and mentors in startup competitions."*
>
> ***Daniel Jamieson, CEO, Biorelate***

If you progress through the stages of a competition, you will likely get expert feedback on both your business plan and your oral pitch. This will help you learn the right language to use and what data and metrics to include when you are pitching to investors. It will also help you start to understand what investors are looking for and how you can stand out from the crowd.

Daniel Jamieson founded his Manchester-based startup company, Biorelate, straight out of graduate school. Daniel and his team of engineers at Biorelate have built a series of software products based on their proprietary machine learning AI. Their products help researchers and companies pull relevant information from published literature, universities and public companies to do competitive analysis and to find collaborators. Daniel entered many business competitions when he was getting Biorelate up and running. He won both the Venture Out and Venture Further Tech Competitions and has since attracted VC funding.

Simon Porphy, CEO and co-founder of MicroSynBiotiX also used both accelerator programs and business competitions for early financing and to connect with mentors, advisors and potential investors. He told me that entering business competitions helped the MicroSynBiotiX team with the funding needed to develop their prototype, helped them form a relationship with a potential market partner and helped them close their seed investment round.

To have the best chance of winning a startup competition, it is a good idea to attend some competitions first and see how the winning entrepreneurs present. Here are just a few of the many biotech and life science business competitions operating around the world.

BIO's Startup Stadium

The Biotechnology Industry Organization (BIO) International Convention is the biggest biotech event in the world. It is an excellent place to network and to learn about competitors, potential partners and current trends in life sciences and healthcare. Startups can apply to be part of their Startup Stadium each year. Finalists are given five to seven minutes to present live to judges and an audience of investors. Unlike the other competitions listed here, it costs $699 to be part of BIO's Startup Stadium. However, this does include access to the BIO One-on-One Partnering program where you can invite any of over 3,500 companies to meet personally with you one-on-one. It usually costs $3,000 to be part of this program so if you are ready to speak with potential partners or investors, this may be a cost-effective way to reach a number of candidates.

MIT $100K

MIT $100K is an entrepreneurship competition open to students and researchers in Boston, Massachusetts. It comprises three separate contests: Pitch, Accelerate and Launch. Semi-finalists share in $300,000 of non-dilutive funding and receive mentorship from venture capitalists, entrepreneurs, industry executives and legal experts.

MedCity Pitch Perfect

MedCity Pitch Perfect is an annual startup contest held at the MedCity INVEST conference in the US. Over 40 startups pitch to judges and investors. Biopharma, diagnostics, medical device, health IT and health services companies are welcome to apply. However, companies must have closed at least one round of funding to be eligible for this competition.

BioStars

BioStars is a UK-based accelerator program and business competition with a prize of £30,000 non-dilutive funding, lab and office space, and mentorship, in the form of workshops and one-on-one meetings. It is run by Panacea Innovation (formerly Oxford Biotech).

HealthTech Challenge

HealthTech Challenge is a business idea competition run by the London Business School. Winners receive mentorship, business training and £10,000. Teams must have at least one postgraduate student or academic researcher to be eligible to enter the HealthTech Challenge.

Biotechnology YES

Biotechnology YES is a business plan competition open to postgraduate students and postdocs in the UK. Students and postdocs attend a three-day workshop with industry mentors where they hone and present a business plan for a hypothetical company. Finalists then present again at a second event and the winner takes home £7,500 and an invitation to attend the BioIndustry Association's annual gala dinner.

European Health Catapult

European Health Catapult is a two-day training program for life science startup entrepreneurs. The training covers topics like writing business plans, negotiating and pitching to investors. Participants also pitch their startup at the training event. 21 finalists are then invited to the EIT Health Summit where they will have more business training and pitch again for the chance to win a share in €135,000.

QuickFire Challenges

Johnson & Johnson's entrepreneurial arm, JLABS, runs a series of competitions called QuickFire Challenges that offer prizes of non-dilutive funding and/or lab space. New challenges are regularly posted for different regions around the world and for different medical applications.

Further Resources

Free online resources where you can find more information about the concepts outlined in this chapter.

BioStars: http://biostars.co/

Biotechnology Industry Organization (BIO)'s Startup Stadium: http://convention.bio.org/startup/

Biotechnology YES: http://www.yescompetitions.co.uk/

European Health Catapult: https://www.europeanhealthcatapult.eu/

HealthTech Challenge: http://www.londonhealthtechchallenge.org/

MedCity Pitch Perfect: https://events.medcitynews.com/invest/pitch-perfect-startup-contest/

MIT $100K: http://www.mit100k.org/

QuickFire Challenges: https://jlabs.jnjinnovation.com/quickfire-challenges

Chapter Nine:
Take Advantage of Community Labs

One of the biggest problems you have when starting a life science company is where to do your experiments. A tech company can start in a garage, or the corner of a lounge room. But life science entrepreneurs need clean lab space and expensive equipment. If you work or study at a university or research institution, any data that you generate at that institution belongs to the institution—even if you do it in your spare time and pay for the reagents. Some institutions even go so far as to claim ownership of all data their employees and trainees create while under contract so make sure you read your employment contract before signing.

You could try and negotiate with your institution to use the premises for set experiments outside of the scope of your official projects and keep ownership of that unofficial data. However, many will not allow you to do that.

That leaves you searching for well-equipped lab space outside of a university or research institution. In major biotech hubs like San Francisco, Boston, Oxford and Cambridge, you can find a range of incubator and accelerator programs dedicated to helping life science startups grow. These programs will often take some equity in exchange for the use of their space and equipment and their business mentorship and networking. Otherwise they charge not insignificant monthly rent for these services. Also, they can be quite picky with who they accept into their programs. I will go over incubators and accelerators in more detail in Chapter Ten.

When you are starting out, you may have little or no money and not enough data to be accepted into an incubator or accelerator program. Community labs are another, more affordable option that could help you do your early proof-of-concept experiments. They usually offer shared office space and internet connection as well as shared lab space.

Community labs have proliferated around the world as the citizen science/DIYbio/biohacking movement continues to grow. Community labs come in all shapes and sizes but most offer shared bench space and laboratory equipment for a low monthly rental fee. Some labs may offer tiered membership. These labs are an affordable option for cash-strapped startups looking to do proof-of-concept experiments or build a prototype. They can also introduce you to a community of biotech entrepreneurs.

Many community labs aim to educate non-scientists about scientific techniques and provide a safe environment where anyone can perform scientific experiments. This means that while community labs are cheap, you do have to share the space with other people which may include non-scientists. This brings up a range of issues such as making sure your reagents aren't used by other people and are stored at the right temperature and that no one interferes with your experiments or has access to your data. Also, very few, if any, community labs will have the capability to do *in vivo* experiments in any models other than bacteria or yeast as it is expensive and time consuming to set up animal facilities that comply with ethical and regulatory requirements.

Most community lab managers will be more than happy to speak with you about ways to mitigate the risks of working within a shared space. They can also help you to apply for government grants such as SBIR grants. You need a physical lab space with enough equipment to be able to run your planned experiments to be eligible for SBIRs and other government grants. It is against the rules of these grants to outsource more than a specific threshold of your work. For example, for SBIR Phase I grants, you can outsource up to 33%.

> *"It's about going lean in the beginning. Capital equipment is expensive. It doesn't make sense to waste money on that."*
>
> ***Jason Poulos, former academic scientist now CEO, Librede***

Jason Poulos is CEO of the synthetic biology company Librede that uses yeast to produce pharmaceutical-grade cannabinoids at a fraction of the cost of growing plants. He chose to conduct early experiments in a community lab so he didn't have to spend money on capital equipment. He also used SBIR grants for early funding and entered pitch competitions to meet investors.

US Community Labs

There are over 40 community labs and DIYbio groups across the US. I've listed a few of them here but you can find many more at www.diybio.org.

Berkeley Biolabs

Berkeley Biolabs is an Environmental Protection Agency (EPA)-compliant co-working lab space in San Francisco. As well as bench space and standard molecular biology equipment, they also offer business mentorship and R&D strategy support. Both companies and individual scientists can join.

BioCurious

BioCurious was the first co-working lab and bio hackerspace to open in the US. It is in Santa Clara in the Bay Area. They run workshops and educational events for the public and are also home to a number of bioentrepreneurs. Membership and use of their shared lab space and molecular biology equipment starts at $100/month or $1000/year.

Bio, Tech and Beyond

Bio, Tech and Beyond is a co-working lab and life science incubator in San Diego. Startup companies can rent a dedicated lab bench with access to shared equipment and basic resources from around $1000/month.

Counter Culture Labs

Counter Culture Labs is a sister lab to BioCurious and is another community biohacking space in the Bay Area. They have standard molecular biology equipment and also offer classes to the public.

GenSpace

GenSpace is a community biolab in Brooklyn, New York. They run classes for the general public ranging from growing your own biotextiles to using CRISPR to genetically engineer organisms. They also offer shared lab space, standard microbiology equipment, disposables and basic reagents from as little as $100 a month. GenSpace is home to several serious bioentrepreneurs. One of their most notable alumni is robotics company Opentrons, which started out at GenSpace and now has 16 employees and has raised over $2 million in private funding.

HiveBio

The HiveBio Community Lab in Seattle has shared lab space and runs classes, citizen projects and student outreach programs.

DIYBio

DIYBio is a network of community lab spaces and biohacker meetup groups across the world. It includes Genspace, HiveBio, Berkeley Biolabs and Bio, Tech and Beyond. You can find a full list of DIYBio groups around the world in the 'Further Resources' section of this chapter.

Europe

It's impractical to list all the community labs in Europe in this book, but here are a few examples.

London Biohackerspace

The London Biohackerspace is a containment level 1 (CL1) biolab based at London Hackspace. For only £2.50/week or £10/month you can access the shared lab space and basic molecular biology equipment.

Biomakespace

Biomakespace is a community lab space in the University of Cambridge, UK dedicated to biology. It opened in January 2018.

Open BioLab Brussels

Open BioLab Brussels is a shared wetlab space located in Brussels, Belgium and open to anyone who wants to learn about biology or run biological experiments. They welcome bioentrepreneurs and startup companies to use their space.

La Paillasse

La Paillasse, the biggest biohacker space in Europe, is in the heart of Paris, France. They run several interdisciplinary scientific projects and are big proponents of open science and open source. While that doesn't fit with a nascent startup's need to protect its IP, if you are in Paris and are in need of lab space, you could speak with the team from La Paillasse about potentially using their space to conduct early experiments.

DIYBio Barcelona

DIYBio Barcelona is an open wetlab in Barcelona. They have a range of classes and collaborative projects and are open to hearing from scientists who could benefit from using their space.

Further Resources

Free online resources where you can find more information about the concepts outlined in this chapter.

Berkeley Biolabs: http://www.berkeleybiolabs.com/

BioCurious: http://biocurious.org/

Biomakespace: https://biomake.space/home

Bio, Tech and Beyond:
https://www.biotechnbeyond.com/

Counter Culture Labs:
http://www.counterculturelabs.org/

DIYBio: https://diybio.org/local/

DIYBio Barcelona: http://www.diybcn.org/

GenSpace: https://www.genspace.org/

HiveBio: http://www.hivebio.org/

La Paillasse: https://lapaillasse.org/

London Biohackerspace: https://biohackspace.org/

Open BioLab Brussels: https://www.openbiolab.be/

Chapter Ten: Apply to Incubator and Accelerator Programs

Life science incubator and accelerator programs offer some combination of lab and office space, business mentorship and connection with advisors and investors. They are the 'grown up' version of community labs and only accept startup companies and bioentrepreneurs, not members of the general public. Incubators and accelerators do not aim to educate the general non-scientific non-entrepreneurial public. Many bioentrepreneurs will start in a community lab, funding their company with government grants, then 'graduate' to an incubator or accelerator program once they have hit early milestones and have proof-of-concept data or an early prototype.

Apart from the obvious benefits of having a place to work, incubators and accelerators also offer the more intangible, but arguably more valuable benefits of letting you tap into an extensive network of experienced biotech entrepreneurs, mentors and investors. Many will coach you on how to write a business plan and build a pitch deck and will then offer you an opportunity to pitch to a room full of investors.

Another benefit of being accepted into an incubator or accelerator program, is that it gives you external validation, much like if you receive a government grant. Investors can see that the group of savvy life science entrepreneurs who run the incubator program have vetted your technology and your team and have decided to accept you into the program.

Overall, these benefits will help you out-compete companies that do not take advantage of an incubator or accelerator program. The 2015 UK Life Science Report by BioCity analyzed data from over 300 life science startups formed in the UK between 2010 and 2014. A little over half (57%) of these companies were in incubators or life science parks. Those companies received, on average, five times more funding than independent companies (£1.9 million versus £0.4 million).

One caveat to the benefits of using an incubator or accelerator is that if you graduate from an incubator without getting funded, investors may see that as a sort of negative validation.

Incubator and accelerator programs are run by all sorts of organizations including private for-profit and not-for-profit companies, big pharma companies, investment firms, real estate companies and state economic agencies. Every program will have its own selection criteria and its own aims and motives. To have the best chance of being accepted, you should look at which companies they have accepted in the past. Most programs will have their alumni or portfolio companies listed on their website. Try to contact these companies to ask for tips or advice on how to apply and also to ask whether they found that incubator or accelerator useful.

US startup incubators and accelerators

There are over 100 life science incubator and accelerator programs in the US. You can find an excellent list at GEN (in the 'Further resources' section of this chapter). I have listed a few of the biggest ones here.

IndieBio

IndieBio is one of the biggest life science accelerator programs in the US. The program is based in San Francisco and offers startups $250,000 in seed funding, access to lab and co-working space and a four-month business boot camp that teaches entrepreneurs how to research their market, develop their product and pitch to investors. These benefits are in exchange for equity in your company—currently 8%. It is a competitive program and you must pitch your startup to IndieBio Directors who will decide whether you make the cut. They have a sister program in Europe called RebelBio. Both IndieBio and RebelBio are part of SOSV, a venture capital fund that focuses on life science startups.

BioLabs

BioLabs is a network of co-working wet lab spaces across the US. They have lab spaces in Boston, New York, San Francisco, San Diego and North Carolina. These are not community labs. Only life science startup companies are accepted into the BioLabs program. Interested entrepreneurs must apply to join and give a 15 to 20-minute presentation to BioLab directors. If accepted, startup companies have access to affordable lab space and to a series of business workshops and networking events. BioLabs alumni have raised over $400 million in private funding. The QB3 incubator space in San Francisco and LabCentral in Boston are both part of the BioLabs Network.

BioHealth Innovation

BioHealth Innovation, based in Rockville, Maryland, runs a series of programs to help bioentrepreneurs secure commercialization grants, learn business basics, find affordable lab space and network with mentors and investors.

Accelerator Corporation

Accelerator Corporation is a biotech investment and management company with physical lab spaces in Seattle, Washington and New York City. Their facilities include offices, meeting rooms and wet lab space. Accelerator was started by biotech investors. Therefore, they offer investment and management advice as part of the package. Their portfolio companies have gone on to raise over $57 million in Series A funding.

Bayer CoLaborator

CoLaborator is incubator space owned and run by Bayer. They have two physical spaces: one next to Bayer's West Coast Innovation Center in San Francisco and one at the R&D Center in Berlin, Germany. Tenants pay market rent for the facilities and are not required to partner with Bayer. Their San Francisco facility is about to grow from 6,000 to 36,000 square feet of office and lab space.

JLABS

JLABS is Johnson & Johnson's startup accelerator arm. They have seven spaces across the US - in San Diego, Boston, San Francisco and Houston - as well as two in Canada - in Toronto and Alberta. They operate under a 'no strings attached' arrangement, whereby tenants pay rent to use the facilities and are not obligated to partner with J&J.

European startup incubators and accelerators

Europe has over 35 life science startup incubators. You can find a list of some of the best at GEN. Here are a few of them.

RebelBio

RebelBio was originally called IndieBio Europe. It is the sister accelerator program to IndieBio and is based in Cork, Ireland. RebelBio offers startups $50,000 in cash and $50,000 worth of resources in exchange for 8% equity. Like IndieBio, it also puts entrepreneurs through a four-month business training program to help them develop their products and pitch to investors.

BioCity Group

The BioCity Group comprises the network of BioCity and MediCity incubators across Northern England and Scotland. They have facilities in Nottingham, Alderley Park and Newhouse, near Glasgow. Their spaces offer both office and lab facilities, as well as business support and mentorship. They also offer investment to some tenant companies. The BioCity program has three stages: Spark; Develop and Launch. Graduate companies from the BioCity Nottingham facility have a 91% survival rate which is almost unheard of in the life science startup world.

Babraham Research Campus

Based in Cambridge, UK, the Babraham Research Campus has research facilities and a range of scientific support services for tenants.

Genopole

Genopole is a cluster of academic life science research labs and startup accelerator facilities in Evry, France (just outside of Paris). They have lab space and also offer business mentorship and coaching services. Genopole companies have raised over €403 million in equity funding.

BioVille

BioVille is a life science and healthcare startup incubator in Diepenbeek, Netherlands with lab and office space, standard equipment and technical and scientific support. They have three buildings designed to house startups at different stages: the Early Development Wing; the Late Development Wing and the Accelerator.

Lund Life Science Incubator

The Lund Life Science Incubator in Sweden has wet labs and office space for biotech startups and also helps with business mentorship and pitching to investors.

Bayer CoLaborator

The CoLaborator incubator spaces in Berlin, Germany and San Francisco, USA are owned and run by Bayer. The German space is at the R&D Center in Berlin. Tenants pay market rent for the facilities and are not required to partner with Bayer.

Further Resources

Free online resources where you can find more information about the concepts outlined in this chapter.

Accelerator Corporation:
http://www.acceleratorcorp.com/

Babraham Research Campus:
http://www.babraham.com/

Bayer CoLaborator:
https://www.colaborator.bayer.com/en/index.php

BioCity: https://www.biocity.co.uk/

BioHealth Innovation:
http://www.biohealthinnovation.org/

BioLabs: https://www.biolabs.io/

BioVille: http://www.bioville.be/en

GEN European Biotech Incubators:
http://www.genengnews.com/the-lists/35-european-biotech-incubators/77900447

GEN US Biotech and Pharma Incubators:
http://www.genengnews.com/the-lists/65-us-biotech-and-pharma-incubators/77900440

Genopole: https://www.genopole.fr/?lang=en

IndieBio: http://indiebio.co/

JLABS: https://jlabs.jnjinnovation.com/

Lund Life Science Incubator: http://www.lundlsi.se/

MediCity: http://www.medicity.com/

RebelBio: https://rebelbio.co/

Chapter Eleven: Incorporate

Incorporation is the legal process of forming a company, or corporate entity. Incorporation allows you to legally run a business and, depending on the corporate structure you choose, gives you some protection against being personally financially responsible for any debts held by the company.

However, the process takes time and money, two things that startup entrepreneurs usually lack. Therefore, it is easy to put off the task of incorporation until it is really necessary. The question is, 'When is it really necessary?'. The answer will depend on your personal circumstances but you cannot receive private funding until you have incorporated.

This chapter will run through why you should incorporate, when to do it and some basic guidelines on how to do it. It does not offer legal or tax advice. While entrepreneurs can bootstrap and DIY many things, I highly recommend you seek professional help for incorporation.

Corporate structures and laws pertaining to incorporation vary from country to country and even from state to state. Regardless of where you choose to do it, you will need to fill in quite a few documents and have a good understanding of the terms that you want to set out for your company, founders and employees. In some countries, such as the US, the UK and France, you can file the required legal documents yourself for a small fee, but it can be easy to miss a crucial step if you are doing it yourself. This could compromise your 'investability'. In other countries, including Belgium, Luxembourg and Germany, only notaries are allowed to file legal documents.

Legal professionals can help you be sure that you have done each step correctly and have set up a company that will be attractive to investors. It is a lot more expensive to use a lawyer than to do it yourself but there are many law firms that are used to working with startup companies who will offer deferred payment deals. This is where the law firm agrees to do upfront legal work for you, up to a certain dollar amount and you need to pay them either by a certain date or when you reach a certain funding milestone.

> *"When you aren't immediately paying for it, it can be hard to keep track of how much everything costs. You may not realize that each email to your lawyers is costing you tens of dollars. Over time this really adds up. Find out how much phone calls,* emails etc. *cost before you send them. Ask other people for advice. You don't have to take every question to your lawyer."*
>
> ***Arshia Firouzi, engineer and CEO of Ravata Solutions***

Ravata Solutions is a startup company in San Francisco creating new technology to generate transgenic animal models. Ravata's co-founders, Arshia Firouzi and Gurkern Sufi, used a deferred payment deal so they could benefit from the assistance of legal professionals without having to pay upfront.

Why Incorporate?

There are a number of reasons why a startup entrepreneur should incorporate his or her company. Before incorporation, you don't actually have a company. You have IP assets.

To receive investment funds

You need to incorporate to receive private equity funding. In this form of funding, cash is exchanged for equity and equity is transferred to investors in the form of shares in the company. This is not possible if the company has not incorporated and issued shares.

One thing to think about at this stage is that investors will want the company to own the IP assets. This means all founders, employees and contractors should transfer any IP ownership to the company at the time of founding. However, if you leave the company for any reason, and this can include being squeezed out by investors, other co-founders or the Board of Directors, you will not own the IP that you may have invented.

To issue cheap shares

Even though, as co-founders, you feel like you should own your company, when you divide equity between co-founders, you do it as company stock and you have to buy this stock. This stock must be purchased at the market value and must be declared as a taxable asset. If you incorporate early, when your company has a low, or no, valuation, you can set the nominal price of your founder stocks at $0.001 per stock. You cannot do this if you choose to incorporate when your company has a valuation of millions of dollars.

To work out equity stakes

As discussed in Chapter Six, working out equity stakes between co-founders can be a very contentious issue. When you incorporate, you must include the equity split between co-founders and any vesting schedule. Once this is done, it costs time and money to re-submit the legal paperwork to change equity ownership. Therefore, you should be sure of the split before incorporating. The act of incorporation can spur co-founders into having this difficult conversation and other problematic conversations about what will happen with company shares should one or more co-founders leave. These terms should be set out in your Founders' Agreement.

For tax purposes

In many countries, including the US, corporate tax rates are lower than personal tax rates, although any dividends you pay yourself are taxed at the dividend tax rate. Also, money may be taxed twice—first as company income, then as personal income. This happens in the case of C corporations in the US. The real tax benefit comes when your company is in the early stages and is not making any money. If you have incorporated, you can write your share of the company losses off on your tax return.

To limit your financial liability

Under most corporate structures, company directors and shareholders are not considered personally liable for any debts incurred by the company, including if you are sued. In the case of substantial debts, you can lose all of your investment in the company but none of your personal assets. If you sign contracts before incorporating, you are signing in your personal name and your financial liability will extend to your personal assets.

Within any corporate structure, founders, directors and CEOs may still be personally liable for any non-compliance with regulatory or tax laws or for any criminal activity.

When should you incorporate?

As soon as you incorporate, you will have to file certain documents and pay fees every year. Therefore, it makes sense to delay this step until it is necessary. There are several scenarios in which it is beneficial to act as a corporation and not an individual.

Before receiving equity funding

As mentioned above, you will need to incorporate before you can receive private equity funding as you will need to transfer equity in the company to investors in the form of shares.

To launch a product or service

Depending on where you live, you may not need to incorporate to be able to sell a product or service, but incorporating will protect you against being personally financially liable if a client or customer sues you.

To sell your business

In the US, if you sell your business as a personal asset, the proceeds are taxed as personal income. If you sell it as a corporation, and you have owned your stock for more than 12 months, the profits will be taxed as capital gains, which is taxed at a lower rate.

Where should you incorporate?

Legal and tax professionals can help you make this decision. The fees to file for incorporation and the ongoing annual fees differ in each state in the US and in each country in Europe. Specific paperwork also differs. Your choice will depend on where you are planning to operate *i.e.* manufacture and sell your product or service. It will also depend on where you are looking to source any investment.

Incorporating in the US

There are more venture capital deals and dollars in the US than in any other country. If you are looking to raise money from American investors, it will help if you base your company in the US. American investors invest in US-based companies more often than in foreign companies. While the lion's share of VC investments go to companies based in the Bay Area, Southern California, Boston and New York, many investors prefer companies that have incorporated in Delaware. Over 50% of all publicly traded companies do so. Corporate attorneys and investors are familiar with Delaware law. The preference for Delaware is because the state has a corporate statute that is business friendly and has a responsive legislature that adapts to the changing business landscape.

Incorporating in Europe

Since Europe is made up of individual countries, it can be harder to decide where to incorporate if you are building a European-based startup rather than an American one. There are quite a few factors to consider when making your choice.

Corporate structures differ between European countries as do set up costs, legal costs and required paperwork. In some countries, such as the UK and France, you can file the paperwork yourself to incorporate your company. In other countries, such as Belgium and Germany, only a notary can file this paperwork. Each country also has its own rules about how many stocks you must issue when you start a company and the nominal value of these stocks.

Each country also has its own tax laws and founder residency laws.

You should also take into account differences in privacy laws. The UK in particular has laws that require companies to publicly disclose financial information, including the names and addresses of company management and directors.

Another factor to consider is the availability of local expertise. If it will be hard to source local employees as your company grows, then you will need to find expatriate workers and may need to help with visa arrangements.

One good way to learn about the differences between European countries is to speak to entrepreneurs who have incorporated in those countries.

What do you need to incorporate?

Each country has different corporate structures and business laws and requires different legal documents to incorporate a business. In this section, I will run through the corporate structures and required documents for American and British companies.

US incorporation

The first step is to decide on a corporate structure for your business. The best option for you depends on whether you want to take outside investment, how many founders you have and how you want to deal with your tax.

Corporate structure

In the US, you can choose to form as a **Limited Liability Company (LLC)**, or incorporate as an **S Corporation (S Corp)** or a **C Corporation (C Corp).** An LLC is technically not a corporation. If you form as an LLC in Delaware, you can easily change to a C Corp later if you choose to do so. There are advantages and disadvantages to each of the three structures.

LLC

Non-US residents can set up an LLC. This structure limits the personal financial liability of owners and has flexible taxation rules—you can elect to be taxed as a sole proprietor, partnership, S Corp or C Corp. LLC may be the best choice for you if your company does not yet need outside investment and is losing money. However, you can't offer stock options to incentivize employees or contractors if you are an LLC. Also, you can't issue shares in an LLC. You need shares to exchange for investment. Therefore, investors do not like to invest in LLCs, they prefer C Corps. For these reasons, some entrepreneurs choose to start as an LLC to protect themselves from personal liability, then change to a C Corp when they start to look for outside investment.

S Corp

An S Corp has special tax status. Choosing to be an S Corp will help you to avoid the double taxation you will face as a C Corp (more on that below). This is because, unlike a C Corp, an S Corp does not pay corporate tax. Employee wages, including company management wages, are taxed at the personal tax rate and other profits are distributed as dividends and taxed at the dividend rate. However, the structure of an S Corp puts restrictions on your equity and capital structure and makes it hard to take outside investment. An S Corp can only have up to 100 shareholders and these can only be 'natural persons' who are US citizens or permanent residents. This means no businesses, institutional investors or foreign investors can provide funding. Also, you can only have one type of stock, which means you cannot issue preferred shares to investors. Many investors will refuse to fund companies if they cannot have preferred shares.

C Corp

A C Corp is the standard corporate structure in the US. C Corp founders and shareholders do not have to be US citizens or permanent residents, although US law prohibits people from certain countries from owning US assets. In a C Corp, the business must file its own tax return and company profits are taxed at the corporate tax rate. If any of the profits go to shareholders as dividends, they are also taxed at the dividend rate. This is the double taxation that is avoided in S Corps. C Corps can issue multiple share types and can create stock options to incentivize employees.

Share classes

In the US, if you incorporate as a C Corp or an S Corp, you can choose to issue different classes of shares, which can have different voting, dividend or capital rights. There are many different classes of shares and you can use these to control the rights of different shareholder groups. Here are some of the most common share classes.

Common or ordinary shares have one vote per share, equal dividend rights and no priority for a cash return when the company exits.

Non-voting shares can be either common or preferred shares but do not carry any voting rights.

Preferred or preference shares usually have preferential dividend rights or guaranteed dividend amounts and priority for a cash return when the company exits. This means that preferred shareholders are paid first both in annual dividends and on exit. Preferred shares may be **cumulative**, meaning that if a company cannot afford to pay dividends one year, this value will accumulate until the company can pay. They may also be **convertible,** so they can be converted to a pre-determined number of common shares at a future date, usually a subsequent funding round. They may also be **callable** or **redeemable** which means that the company may or will buy them back at a fixed price at or by a certain date or milestone. *Note: the exact rights carried by preferred shares is a compromise between investors and the company, as investors will always want more rights and companies will always want to limit these rights.*

Founders' shares are issued at the time of incorporation for a nominal price - often $0.001 per share. These are usually common shares, although they can be preferred. Founders may choose to confer specific rights to this class of shares. Be wary of doing this as it may make investors less inclined to invest in your company. Founders' shares are often vested, so founders will receive a certain percentage of shares over a period of time or when the company meets certain milestones.

Stock options give recipients the right to purchase shares for a set price (the **exercise price**). Stock options can be used to incentivize employees, directors and consultants in place of cash remuneration. Like stock, options can be vested so they will only become available after an employee or consultant has worked for the company for a certain amount of time or has achieved certain milestones. Options can be very valuable if the market value of the company stock becomes much higher than the exercise price. If you want to be able to issue stock options, you will need to set aside an option pool when you divide up the equity among founders. Many people choose to keep 10-20% aside as options.

Note: the cash value of any shares, regardless of class, is considered taxable income.

Required Documents to Form or Incorporate

These are slightly different depending on whether you choose to form as an LLC or incorporate (as either an S Corp or C Corp) and depending on which state you choose to incorporate in. These are the documents you will likely need to incorporate in the US.

	Corporation	**LLC**
Formation	Articles of Incorporation	Articles of Formation
Ownership	Share Certificate for each shareholder	Member Ccrtificate for each member
Governance	Shareholder Agreement and Bylaws	Operating Agreement
Tax	Apply for an Employer Identification	Apply for an Employer Identification

	Number – IRS Form SS4	Number – IRS Form SS4
Founders	Founders' Agreement	Founders' Agreement
Confidentiality	Non-Disclosure Agreement	Non-Disclosure Agreement
Employment and non-compete	Employee Agreement	Employee Agreement

Articles of Incorporation or Formation

Specific requirements of the Articles of Incorporation depend on the state in which you incorporate but most will require the following:

- Name and business address of the corporation
- Number and value of any shares issued
- Name and address of the registered agent (a responsible third party in the state in which you incorporate who can act as a contact person between your business and the state)
- Names and addresses of incorporators (co-founders)
- Names and addresses of any directors
- The purpose of the corporation

Non-Disclosure Agreements

You will need to share confidential information about your IP and business with employees, mentors and contractors. To make sure that these people do not share that information, you should have them sign a non-disclosure agreement (NDA). These can also be called confidential disclosure agreements (CDAs), which are essentially the same thing.

You can't make everyone you talk to about your business sign an NDA. Investors will not sign an NDA until late in the due diligence process. Therefore, you do need to get used to sharing only non-confidential information when initially pitching your company or speaking about your IP to other entrepreneurs or potential mentors.

Founders' Agreement

The Founders' Agreement is not required to incorporate in the US. However, almost every entrepreneur and mentor I have spoken with highly recommends writing a Founders' Agreement when you start a company. This document will set out any terms that the founders have agreed upon. It is a legally binding document so can help avoid any future arguments if business development doesn't go as planned. Consider including the following in your Founders' Agreement:

- Roles and responsibilities. Who will be CEO? What will other titles be? What are each person's responsibilities? Everyone working in a startup needs to be able to wear multiple hats, but it is inefficient to have everyone working on everything. Responsibilities and day-to-day tasks need to be assigned to different people.
- Equity split. Assign equity to each co-founder and include a vesting schedule. Also include terms on what will happen to that equity should a co-founder choose to leave the company or be forced out of the company by other co-founders.

- Assign any IP rights to the company. For investors to be interested in the company, the company itself must own the IP rights.
- Non-compete and confidentiality clauses. You want to make sure that none of the co-founders can work for competing companies or share any confidential information.

Employee Agreements

Employee Agreements are also not essential documents when incorporating. However, like Founders' Agreements, these documents can set out the roles and responsibilities of each employee and include important non-compete and confidentiality clauses. It is worth thinking about using such agreements from the beginning to protect your IP and your competitive advantage.

Record keeping

Once you form an LLC or incorporate as an S Corp or a C Corp, you are legally required to keep certain records. Exact requirements depend on the state in which you incorporate but all states require some version of the following records.

- A **share register**, which is a record of the number and classes of all shares you have issued as well as details on all shareholders - their names and addresses, dates they acquired shares and how many shares of each class they own.
- Full financial and tax records. This will be easiest if you open a bank account in the company's name and do not use any personal bank accounts.
- Up-to-date versions of any amendments to your articles or organization.

UK Incorporation

Any one over the age of 16 can set up a company in the UK. You do not have to be a UK citizen or resident, but the company must have a registered office in the UK. If you do not have access to a UK address for your company, you can use a Registration Agency Service.

The most common corporate structure for UK startups is the Private Limited Company (Ltd). A Ltd company is legally separate from company managers and has separate company finances. All Ltd companies must have a registered office in the UK, at least one director, one shareholder and one share issued at time of incorporation. Your company name also has to abide by certain rules—it cannot be offensive or be too similar to another registered company name.

You can register your company online for only £12 if you use the Standard Articles of Association, also called Model Articles.

You need the following documents and information to incorporate as a Ltd in the UK:

- Company name and address
- Director/s name/s and address/es
- Statement of Capital listing the number and type of all issued shares, including details on dividend and voting rights, whether the shares are redeemable, and the names and addresses of all shareholders
- Standard industrial classification of economic activities (SIC) classification of your company
- Memorandum and Articles of Association
- Details of 'people with significant control' of your company *i.e.* anyone with more than 25% shares or voting rights

Memorandum of Association

The Memorandum of Association is a document signaling that initial shareholders (called subscribers in this context) intend to form a new company limited by shares, that the subscribers will become members of that company and will each own at least one share. Make sure this document is correct, as it cannot be amended after you register your company.

Articles of Association

The Articles of Association are the rules and bylaws of the company that all company officers must follow.

To register online, you have to use the standard articles of association, called the model articles. If you want to customize these, or write your own articles, you cannot register online and will need to use an agent.

Note: This is a publicly available document. All names and addresses of directors, the company secretary and shareholders are also available to the public. However, directors can apply to the UK companies register, called Companies House, to keep their addresses confidential.

Tax

You must register to pay corporation tax within three months of incorporating.

Record Keeping

UK limited companies must submit a Confirmation Statement and Annual Accounts to Companies House and HM Revenue and Customs (HMRC) at least once a year.

The Confirmation Statement has current company details including company name and address and details of company directors, secretary and shareholders, along with any People with Significant Control (who own more than 25% of the company shares or voting rights). It also contains details of issued shares and share value.

The Annual accounts should include:

- Profits and losses *i.e.* all monies received and paid by the company
- Balance sheet detailing all assets and liabilities (debts—both owed and owing), all goods bought and sold, and any stocks held by the company
- A director's report
- An auditor's report, unless your company is exempt

Seedsummit

Seedsummit is a group of 25 investors who have created and posted templates of legal documents for startups in the UK, Hong Kong and Portugal. These templates are free to download and use.

Further Resources

Free online resources where you can find more information about the concepts outlined in this chapter.

Classes of shares:
http://www.companylawclub.co.uk/classes-of-shares

Company House (UK):
https://www.gov.uk/government/organisations/companies-house

Incorporation and names – Guidance from the UK Government:
https://www.gov.uk/government/publications/incorporation-and-names/incorporation-and-names

Internal Revenue Service Business Structures:
https://www.irs.gov/businesses/small-businesses-self-employed/business-structures

Legal Tips for Startups:
http://lifesciencenetwork.com/blogs/lsn-editorial-team/2017/03/06/legal-tips-for-startups

Seedsummit: http://seedsummit.org/

Set Up a Private Limited Company (UK):
https://www.gov.uk/limited-company-formation

The 10 Key Legal Documents for Your Business:
https://www.entrepreneur.com/article/236967

Chapter Twelve: Market Like a Scientist

When you are a startup entrepreneur, you are busy building a product, platform or service, building a company, managing people and chasing investment. You don't have time to worry about marketing. That can come later when you have a product and a marketing budget.

That's not true.

Marketing refers to all facets of creating and delivering an application to a customer. This means that marketing should be interwoven into every part of your company. You start with market analysis to understand your target market - to gather deep knowledge of the number, wealth and buying habits of your future customers, but more importantly to understand the problems they face and how you can solve these problems. Marketing also includes competitive analysis. Only by understanding your industry and the strengths and weaknesses of your competitors, can you work out how to create an application that better solves the problem of your target customers. You use the knowledge gained from your market analysis and competitive analysis to design and build an application with the best product/market fit possible. Investors want to see product/market fit. They also want to see a marketing plan, however basic, in your investor pitch.

The whole time you are developing your application, you need to be also building a company **brand**. People will only use a product or service that:

1. They know about
2. They trust

This knowledge or trust may come through a trusted referral. For example, when a doctor prescribes medication for a patient, many patients will take that medication without questions because they trust their doctor. Likewise, an investor is more likely to meet with startup entrepreneurs if they are introduced by someone whom the investor trusts.

For the trusted referral system to work for your company, you need referrers, such as doctors or other entrepreneurs, to know about your company and believe in your application. These people are also called **company evangelists**.

The only way to find company evangelists is to build a strong brand. And you build a strong brand through a combination of **public relations** (PR) and marketing.

At a startup, one person may be responsible for all marketing, PR, sales and business development, among other responsibilities, until you grow and can afford to hire more staff. While these four areas are all intertwined, and have the ultimate goal of bringing in revenue, they each approach that goal in a different way. It is important to understand these differences as you grow and look to hire new people. You can avoid a lot of problems by having clearly defined roles and responsibilities from the very beginning of your life as a company.

Marketing, PR, Sales and Business Development

Marketing *refers to building and delivering an application to a customer. It encompasses all communication with actual and potential customers.*

Public relations (PR) *refers to creating awareness of your company and product by communicating with, and building relationships with, all other audiences. This includes investors, partners, employees, end-users and the general public.*

Sales *is about closing the actual transaction where money is exchanged for goods or services. Sales staff will have specific sales targets.*

Business development *is about developing partnerships to help your company grow. This includes corporate partners, investors, supporters such as patient advocacy groups and large or corporate customers. Both marketing and business development will find and nurture* ***leads*** *(potential customers) and pass them to the sales team when the potential customers are ready to buy.*

Market like a scientist

Data-driven marketing is the most effective marketing. Simply put, if something works, keep doing it. If something doesn't work, stop doing it and switch to something else. The only way you will know what worked and what didn't is to approach marketing like a scientific experiment.

Set up experiments with defined goals and metrics

↓

Measure results through repeatable, meaningful metrics

↓

Record results to show any growth

↓

Revise

↓

Refine

↓

Repeat

You can set up this sort of testing with every aspect of your marketing plan. More on this in the 'Marketing Plan' section later in this chapter.

When to start marketing

You may want to operate in **stealth mode** while you are developing your product, particularly if it is first-in-class, so that competitors don't know what you are doing. Also, you probably won't have a big marketing budget when you first start your company. These are two good reasons not to do a lot of marketing.

However, you should still use marketing principles to analyze your target market and research your target customers and your competitors. You should also use marketing and PR principles to start building awareness of your company and your brand. It takes years to establish yourself, or a company spokesperson, as a **key opinion leader** and to develop relationships with the media, influencers, partners and investors. Successful business relationships are based on trust and it takes time to earn that trust.

You need to start that process when you start your company.

Market analysis

When you analyze your target market, you are looking to understand the size of this market as well as any factors that affect the buying power or habits of this market. This includes nationality, geographical location, health insurance status, disposable income, age, sex, online and offline information consumption and buying habits, and product design preferences.

Customer lifetime value

The customer lifetime value estimates the net profit that a customer will bring your company over the lifetime of their relationship with you. Your profit margin is the amount that customer spends on your product or service minus the amount of money it costs you to create your product and sell it to that customer. You won't keep 100% of your customers, so you need to factor in your ***retention rate****, or how many customers you will keep over a certain time period. The inverse of your retention rate is your* ***churn rate****, which is how many customers you lose.*

Here is a simple formula to calculate CLVs:
Customer lifetime value ($) = Average monthly profit margin per customer *x* Average customer lifespan in months

For example, if you have a new drug to treat multiple sclerosis that costs each patient $5,000 per month and your profit margin is $2,000 per patient per month and, on average, customers continue to take your drug for 15 months, then your CLV = $2,000 x 15 = $30,000. You can use this value to set a budget for marketing and building a sales team to deliver your product or service to your customers.

More complicated formulas take into account the ***discount rate,*** *which is the cost to acquire future sales from a customer.*

You need to know who your target customers are, how they like to consume information and how you can get information about your product to them. You also need to know how much they can and will pay for your proposed application. Lastly, you must estimate how many target customers you have, how much it will cost you to get to each one and how much net profit each customer will bring to the company - the **customer lifetime value.**

Market size

There are two main approaches to calculating market size, which I outlined in Chapter One. They are the top down or bottom up methods.

If you don't partner with a bigger company to market your product, you will probably have to stage your market approach. For example, you may aim to target Type 2 Diabetes patients in the US first, then expand to the European market, then Asia, then the rest of the world. You should calculate the size of each of these markets and estimate the marketing costs to reach these markets.

Top down market sizing

In top down market analysis, you estimate the total dollar value of a market, then calculate how much of that market you can reach *i.e.* the value of your market share. You can use census data, market reports and statistics gathered by the World Health Organization, as well as published academic literature, to estimate your total market size or total addressable market. To then work out how much of that market you can convert to using your product, called your obtainable market, you need to know how many competitors have similar products, how much those products sell for, how many customers use each product and how your product is different and better.

For example, according to a report by BCC Research, the continuous glucose monitoring market is estimated to be worth $784 million by 2019. If you are developing a continuous glucose monitoring device, and your device is significantly better than competitor devices, you may be able to reach 20% of that market. You may be able to reach 30% of the market. You will never reach 100% of the market, and the share that you do reach will depend on how many competing devices are on the market, how yours is different and better, the pricing of each device and how much money you can spend on marketing.

Angel and VC investors like to see a market size of at least $1 billion to invest in a company. In the case of blood glucose monitoring, most Type 2 Diabetes patients use blood glucose meters to monitor their blood glucose levels because these are cheaper than continuous glucose monitoring devices and are covered by most health insurers and other payers. The blood glucose meter market is predicted to be worth over $16 billion by 2019. If you have a reasonable plan to convert a portion of this market to your new continuous glucose monitoring device, you could dramatically increase your estimated target market.

Your plan must be reasonable and you must have evidence to back it up, such as cost comparisons, customer surveys and testimonials. In this glucose monitoring example, you would need survey data from both the patient, who is the end-user, and testimonials from the customer, who is the insurance company or national healthcare provider.

Bottom up market sizing

The bottom up approach to market sizing is based on defining your target customer. Then you calculate the number of these potential customers, how many of these people you can reach and how much each sale is worth.

> *Market size = number of customers x market penetrance x average sale value*

Do customer interviews and create customer personas to define your target customer. Use census data and data from the WHO, the NIH and patient support groups as well as published academic literature and market research reports to estimate the number of your potential customers.

Your **market penetrance** is the percentage of your potential market that you can reach. This percentage is your obtainable market. Your market penetrance depends on the visibility of your product, which in turn depends on the success of your PR and marketing campaigns. You should have detailed PR and marketing plans to reach your target market. These plans must have specific milestones and budgets. Investors will want to see this in your pitch.

To calculate an average sales value, you will need to look at comparable sales of competing products and understand the acceptable price points for your target customers. You can get this information from competitive analysis and by doing surveys and interviews with customers and end-users. Depending on what sort of application you are developing, this could mean talking to patients, physicians, hospitals, insurance companies or national healthcare systems such as the NHS in the UK or Medicare in Australia. For example, if competitors A, B and C sell continuous glucose monitoring devices for $382.50, $495.00 and $270.56, respectively, and they are all covered by insurance plans, then you could project that you could sell your device for at least $270.

Reimbursement

Reimbursement is a key issue for life science companies developing pharmaceuticals, medical devices or diagnostic tests. It is less important for companies developing laboratory equipment or non-clinical software. The term reimbursement refers to whether or not an insurance company or national healthcare provider (a payer) will pay for all or part of a product or service. If payers will not cover your drug, medical device or diagnostic, you will find it very difficult to sell. Therefore, reimbursement affects your market penetrance. It also affects your pricing as payers will set the maximum amount they are willing to pay for your product.

You should take reimbursement into account in any product development and marketing plans. You can search for reimbursement codes yourself on the Centers for Medicare and Medicaid (CMS) website in the US, or hire reimbursement consultants or an agency to do this for you. These codes will show you if similar products are covered by payers in your country and the reimbursement amount for comparable products.

In Europe, each country is responsible for deciding which pharmaceuticals and medical devices it will cover under its national healthcare or social security system, and for setting the price for each product. You can find more information on EU pricing and reimbursement on the European Commission website.

I go over reimbursement in more detail in Chapter Four.

Competitive analysis

To calculate an accurate market size and create a viable reimbursement strategy, you need to understand the competitive landscape. If you know what customers do and don't like about your competitors' products, it will help you design an application with good product/market fit and will help you come up with strategies to convert their customers to your product or service. Also, you can analyze your competitors' marketing strategies to see what does and doesn't work with your target market.

You need to know how many companies have applications similar to yours. You should develop a profile for each company and each product. Lastly you should put all of these companies or products into a graphic such as a matrix for your investor pitch deck.

With your competing company profiles, you want to understand how many products or services each company has and what their R&D and marketing budgets are. This will give you an idea of how important each product is to them, how rigorously they will defend their market share and what resources they have to do so. You also want to know what products they have in development. Academic papers and conference proceedings, as well as press releases, can help you work this out.

> *Investors have a good understanding of your industry and your competitors.*
>
> *They want to know that you also have a thorough understanding and have a plan to mitigate the risk from competition.*

To get insights into how each company reaches its target customers, sign up to their email lists and follow on them social media. This will help you learn how your target customers respond to different media channels and different messages.

Customer persona

A customer persona, also called a **customer avatar** is a description of the buying habits and behavior of your target customer. The customer is the person who pays for the product or service. The end-user is the person who uses the product or service. Your customers may or may not be your end-users. To successfully market, you need to convince both groups of the value of your product. However, if you convince the customer of the value, they may help to convince the end-user.

A life science customer may be a patient, a doctor or other healthcare provider, a hospital, a health insurance company or a national healthcare system. Regardless of who your customer is, you should research their wealth (income or revenue or budget) and their spending habits. You may have more than one type of customer or end-user per product.

For example, if you are developing a new surgical implant that surgeons can use in fracture repair, how many hospitals (customer) currently buy this type of implant? Are these hospitals small, medium-sized or large? How much do they spend on these types of implants? How many surgeons (end-users) choose this type of implant and can perform this type of surgery? Do any insurance companies (customer) cover this type of implant? How much do they pay? How many patients (customer and end-user) need this sort of surgery? What is their disposable income? How likely are they to pay a gap for this sort of implant, rather than choose a cheaper option? You need to understand how much of the cost of the implant is covered by the insurance company versus the patient. You also need to understand the sales and reimbursement cycles of the product. Does the hospital buy the implant from you first and then ask for reimbursement from the insurer? How long does this take? From which budget does the hospital buy surgical consumables?

Customer interviews

Customer interviews and surveys will help you build your customer persona or avatar. They will help you understand the price ranges for your product that your target customers find acceptable. More importantly, they help you understand what sorts of problems your customer faces and how they currently solve those problems. You will find out what they do and don't like about the current solutions to their problems and what their ideal solution would entail. You can also get a feel for which side effects of a treatment or diagnostic are acceptable and which are not. All of this information will help you to build a product with a good product/market fit. Without that, you will not be able to attract investment and you will not be able to bring in a healthy revenue stream.

Segmentation

As mentioned above, you may have more than one type of customer. These customers may have very different incomes and buying habits and consume their information in different ways. Therefore, you need to employ different tactics to reach your different customers. You also need to direct different messages to each audience. This is called **customer segmentation**. Each message should speak about the problem faced by that particular customer type. For example, a surgeon may want to cut down surgical time to decrease the incidence of surgical complications. For a patient, the main concern may not be the duration of the actual surgery, but more how long it takes to recover from the surgery. Your product may provide a superior solution to both these problems but the way you present that information to a surgeon and a patient will use different wording and graphics. In another example, the same surgical implant may be used in patients who are 20 to 30 years old as well as patients who are 60 to 80 years old. These two groups will use very different information sources. They will also respond to different language. You need to craft your message differently to each group.

Segmentation will help you conduct appropriate A/B testing and other experiments to test and refine your marketing and PR plans.

> ***A/B testing***
>
> *A/B testing is a simple experiment where you test two different conditions to see which performs better. For example, you might send a marketing email with one subject line to half the people on your email list, and use another subject line in the email sent to the other half. Then you measure the open and click rates for each condition to see which subject line performed better.*

Product/Market Fit

Investors want to see good product/market fit. This means that the product or service you are creating genuinely solves a problem for your target market and therefore, the market will adopt the new application. It doesn't matter if your technology is amazing and your product is the fastest/most efficient/most effective if it costs too much to make or if your target market doesn't want it.

In life sciences, reimbursement is a big part of product/market fit. It means nothing if your FDA-approved therapeutic is more effective and has less side effects than competing drugs if insurance companies will not cover it.

Build your brand

Your brand is the essence of your company. It is how customers recognize, trust and know what to expect from your company and your products or services.

You can have both a personal and a company brand. Every professional interaction you have, both online and in the real world, contributes to both your personal and your company brand. Something as simple as a tweet can influence how people view your company. You should be mindful of this from the moment you sign up to a new social media platform or send an email or design a company website. Everything you do should work towards building awareness of, and trust in, yourself and your company. Word-of-mouth referrals are one of the most powerful

What's in a name?

Mark Fortner is founder and CTO at Aspen Biosciences. The Aspen team chose their name "not only because it aligns with our mission, but also because it invites inquiry, and the explanation tends to make the company name memorable. At Aspen Biosciences, we write software to help drug discovery and cancer research organizations 'connect the dots'. We get our name from the Pando aspen forest in southern Utah. This forest is a clonal colony of trees, and as such, represents the world's largest single living organism. It's root system allows the trees to communicate biochemically with one another, similar to the way in which the cells of a brain communicate. Similarly, we help our customers pull together data from disparate parts of their organization, to give them a more holistic view of their projects."

forms of marketing and this will only come if people trust you.

Brand basics

The most basic parts of your company brand are your company name and logo. Your name should be professional and not offensive, convey what your company does and differentiate you from other companies.

Erik Clausen is a managing partner at the life science marketing firm CG Life. He recommends that startup companies "choose a name that can be used to tell a story. There should be a back story with any selected name and that story should map to or convey the organization's core messages or values."

Before choosing a name, you should check that it hasn't been trademarked by someone else, that the url is available, preferably as name.com and the name is available on social media platforms.

Each country has an intellectual property office, such as the United States Patent and Trademark Office (USPTO) or the European Union Intellectual Property Office. Many of these have trademark databases that you can search online to make sure that your proposed company name is available. If your name is available in every country in which you wish to operate, you can usually apply for a trademark using the same websites for a small fee.

Your logo is a visual representation of your company. It should immediately differentiate you from other companies. A good logo is related to what your company does and avoids colors or images that are offensive in any of your target markets. These factors will be different in different countries. For example, yellow can be associated with pornography in China. In Latin America, yellow may be associated with death and mourning. Six degrees has a useful chart of international color symbolism that might help when you are designing your logo. Lastly, you want to keep in mind the printability and scalability of your logo and how it appears both online and in print form.

If you don't know any graphic designers who can help you with your logo, you can find freelancers on websites like Upwork and fiverr.

Value proposition

Your brand is about much more than your company name and logo. It is also about what makes you different and better than competitors.

The **value proposition** is your unique selling point. It is a short statement that explains why a customer should buy your product or use your service. A value prop should include the problem you are addressing, your solution and why you are better than competitors. Another term used to describe this is **killer app**. Your killer app is the core value of your technology that makes you better than competitors and attractive to customers.

Your value proposition can be distilled into a **tagline**, ten or less words that explain the core of who you are and what you do. A tagline should be easy to remember and show at a glance what your company does. Some examples of life science startup taglines:

- Ravata Solutions: Production Scale Embryo Engineering
- MicroSynbiotiX: Oral Vaccination—Disease Management for Aquaculture
- MamaStrut: OB/GYNs and Moms Agree that MamaStrut is the #1 Post Birth Care System
- AxoSim: Human data, faster.

Use your value proposition to define **keywords** to use on your website and in marketing material.

> ***Keywords***
>
> *Keywords are the words or phrases that people use when searching the internet. You can use tools like Google AdWords to work out the most relevant keywords that relate to your application. You want to pick the keywords that are the most popular but have the least competition. It is almost impossible for a startup to compete on keywords with giants like Thermo Fisher Scientific or Roche. Once you have chosen keywords, you should include them in your website pages and blog posts to improve your website ranking in search engines for those terms.*

Company mission

You don't have to include a company mission, vision or core values in a pitch or in a marketing plan. However, if you take the time to write these things down, they will help you define who you are as a company and can also help you to keep on track as your company grows and evolves. Taking the time to understand your company will help you build a strong brand.

Your **company mission** is different to your value proposition. Your value prop is an external statement telling the world why they should buy your product or use your service. Your company mission is an internal statement reminding all company management, advisors, investors, mentors and employees what your core mission is and what you are all working to achieve. It is a statement about what your company does. You should use your company mission to draft company goals and create your company culture. Everything you do as a leader in your company should stay true to your company mission.

Company vision

Your **company vision** is different to your mission because it explains what you want your company to become e.g. the leading cancer diagnostic company.

Core Values

Your core values are the principles, beliefs and philosophy that you want to maintain within your company. The core values underpin the culture you want your company to have. They are the standards by which you expect all employees to work and interact.

Company goals

Your company mission, vision and values should stay fairly fixed, unless you make major pivots. However, your company goals will change as you grow and achieve each goal and milestone. You should be specific when you set goals and include a time frame within which you want to achieve each goal. You should also measure and record the results and metrics associated with each goal.

> ***Pivot***
>
> *A pivot is a fundamental change in your business. This change can be related to your product, your target customer or the way your business is set up.*

SWOT Analysis

A SWOT analysis looks at the Strengths, Weaknesses, Opportunities and Threats of your company. It makes you think about whether your products really are different and better than competitors. You need to be brutally honest for this analysis to help you. List three to five core strengths and weakness of your company and follow up with your three to five main opportunities and threats. You can apply this analysis to your whole company and to each of your products or services. Do the same for each of your competitors. If your SWOT analysis shows you that you don't have a strong competitive advantage, the best move is to rethink your product development plans and business strategy rather than continue to push ahead on your current path.

Have a professional website

Your website is one of the first places people will go to get information about your company. If you don't have a website, you look unprofessional. If you have a poorly designed website with no real information, you look unprofessional.

Website hosting platforms

It takes a lot of coding to build a website from scratch. You may want to do that if you are building an online community or platform or creating digital health software. If not, there are a number of website hosting platforms that make it quick and easy to set up a website, including WordPress, Wix, Weebly and Squarespace. These platforms charge a low annual fee to host your website and will charge an additional fee if you want to personalize your domain name. This is well worth the extra cost.

Domain name

You want a domain name that relates to your company and is easy to remember. Ideally it should be 'yourcompanyname.com'. For this reason, when choosing a company name, you should look at available domain names by typing your candidates into search engines or using a domain search tool such as GoDaddy. You may find that someone owns your desired domain name but is not using it. In that case, you can contact the owner through a domain search tool and negotiate a price to buy the domain name.

Website content

Your website is often the first thing people see from your company. It is your one chance to make a good first impression. Therefore, it needs to be well laid out and easy to read. Website hosting platforms have many different default layouts from which you can choose so you don't have to do this yourself. Play around with the options and decide which looks best. Ask friends and colleagues for their feedback.

A life science website is a science communication tool. As with any other communication tool, you should follow some basic rules when creating the content for your website:

- Use clear, simple language
- Tell a story
- Explain why your technology is better
- Introduce your team members and show their strengths
- Use graphics, images and videos where possible to illustrate your points

An early-stage life science company has three main audiences: investors; potential partners and customers. Each of these groups is looking for different information. Investors want to see an elevator pitch - what problem you solve for whom, the size of your market, evidence of good product/market fit and an explanation of why you are better than competitors. Potential partners want to understand your science and your product pipeline and see how it fits into their pipeline and strategy. Customers want to know how you are solving their problem, see evidence that you have solved the problem for other people (building trust) and learn where they can buy your product or service.

The difference between a product and a pipeline

A pipeline comprises any products a company is developing. The products can be at difference stages of development and have different indications. For example, Arrowhead Pharmaceuticals is developing drug candidates based on RNA-interference for diverse diseases including Hepatitis B, Renal Cell Carcinoma and Cardiovascular Disease.

A company with more than one product in their pipeline might be more attractive to investors than a company with only one application under development. Unless, of course, the company with one product is developing a novel product with good product/market fit that solves an unmet medical need for a large patient population.

It is very difficult to fit all the necessary information for these three different audiences on your homepage, therefore you should direct the different audiences to a page specifically designed for them by having a clickable image, box, tab or link for 'Investors', 'Partners' and 'Patients' or 'Physicians/Providers'.

Your homepage should be simple with an image, your value proposition and obvious links to find further information *e.g.* 'About', 'Technology', 'Products' or 'Pipeline'. Also include any patient/customer testimonials and any positive coverage by media outlets. This **third-party validation** helps build trust.

The about page should include key information about your company and your team. People want to see the faces behind the company and know your experience and credentials. This is very important to building trust. No one will trust a company if they do not know who is running it.

The technology page should use simple language and non-proprietary information to explain how your technology works and how it is better than competing technologies.

The product or pipeline page should have a simple graph showing how far along the development timeline you are with each product. The graph should have clickable links taking people to a new page with more information about each product and the problem it addresses.

Two examples of well designed, informative biotech websites are synthetic biology company Synthorx: www.synthorx.com and RNA medicine company Arrowhead Pharmaceuticals: www.arrowheadpharma.com.

Regulatory and legal concerns

Life science companies must comply with legal and regulatory guidelines on how to market and sell products. If your company is still private *i.e.* you have not made an initial public offering (IPO), you cannot publicly solicit for investment. Therefore, your website must be carefully worded to avoid offering an investment opportunity. Instead, you can invite any interested investors and partners to contact you. Likewise, regulatory bodies such as the FDA have strict rules on how you can describe a product that has not yet been approved. You cannot call any new pharmaceutical under development a 'drug'. You must use the term 'drug candidate'.

If you collect any patient data, such as contact details of anyone interested in news about your product development, you have to abide by HIPAA (Health Insurance Portability and Accountability Act of 1996) and HITECH (Health Information Technology for Economic and Clinical Health) regulations in the US and the General Data Protection Regulation (GDPR) in the EU. I go through this in more detail in Chapter Four.

SEO

Search Engine Optimization (SEO) refers to using techniques to boost your ranking on internet search engines. The first step is choosing keywords - words that your target audience uses to search for companies or products/services like yours. You want keywords with high traffic but low competition. Choosing something like 'biotech' will not help because so many other people have chosen that term and optimized their web content to rank highly for that term.

Long tail keywords are short phrases that specifically describe your product. You might be better off choosing to optimize your content for a couple of long tail keywords rather than going for the popular terms like 'biotech' or 'cancer'. For example, if you are developing an RNA-interference medicine for cancer, you could choose the long tail keyword 'RNA medicine cancer'. You need to keep your target audience in mind when choosing keywords. Make sure your keywords aren't so technical that investors or customers wouldn't use them.

There are free online tools like Google AdWords that you can use to search for keywords and to see the traffic that each keyword combination attracts. You can also enter those keywords into search engines to see what comes up. That will show you who is ranking for those keywords.

To rank highly on a search engine for a particular keyword, you need to use that keyword in your content (several times, but not too often and never out of context). Using the same keyword too many times is called keyword stuffing and is penalized by search engines. A good rule of thumb is to use a keyword no more than two to three times per 100 words of content. You can include several different related keywords in your content. Ideally, you also want to include your keywords in your url. If you have a blog on your website, it is easy to do this.

You also need to have backlinks to your site if you want to rank highly on a search engine. A backlink is when another website links to your site. The best way to get backlinks is to guest blog for other sites and to get media coverage from journalists and bloggers.

If this sounds like a lot of work, it is. But it will help you stay ahead of competitors if you are more visible that they are on the web.

Public Relations

Public relations or PR refers to all communication strategies to build awareness of your brand and to develop relationships with investors, partners, the media and the general public. If you start PR early, and many people are aware of your company and your product by the time you launch, it will be much easier to convert people into customers.

Paid vs Owned vs Earned media

Paid media *is any media you pay for. This includes print, TV and radio advertisements, pay per click ads, social media ads and promoted posts, search engine ads and promoted listings and some contributed articles or editorials in trade publications or other media outlets.*

Owned media *is any media that you create on a channel that you own. This includes any content on your website, email marketing, eBooks, white papers, videos and social media posts.*

Earned media *is media that you did not pay for and you did not create. It is media created by an independent person like a journalist. It is often the most powerful form of media because it comes with inherent* ***third party validation*** *i.e. someone other than you is talking about your company or product. This is always more believable than when you talk about yourself.*

Investor Relations

One of the most important facets of PR for an early-stage life science company is investor relations. Before you have a product or service ready to sell, investors are essentially your target customers. In Chapter Thirteen, I go through how to decide when to approach investors and whom to approach. In Chapter Fourteen, I talk about how to pitch to investors and provide a template for the all-important pitch deck.

Investors make investments based on trust. They need to hear about you from someone they trust and you need to show them that your team can develop an application that solves a true need for a big market. Both these things take time. Whenever you communicate anything about your life science startup, keep in mind how investors will view your company. Make sure your website, pitch deck, executive summary, brochures and social media accounts are all professional, send the same clear message and align with your brand.

Investor relations also refers to getting to the investors. Usually this means finding someone they trust to introduce you. The only way to do that is to expand your own professional network and build and deepen relationships with well-connected individuals. You can do this by entering business competitions, attending pitch nights and networking events and applying to community labs, incubators and accelerators.

Media relations

The media, whether it is traditional media, such as newspapers, television and radio, or 'new' media like blogs and YouTube videos, is one of the best ways to tell people about your company and your products or services. You can pay for ads but 'earned' or 'free' media is more effective at earning the trust of your target audience and converting them into customers. It is also free, unlike ads, which can be very expensive.

However, earned media takes time. You need to build relationships with journalists and prominent bloggers so they will cover your company

> ***HARO***
>
> *HARO (Help A Reporter Out) is a free platform that links journalists and sources. You can sign up and select your areas of interest and you will receive an email three times a day with journalists asking for sources for particular stories. You can get positive media coverage even before you have company news by using this approach.*

news. One way to do this is to reach out to writers early and offer yourself as an expert in your sector.

Pitching to reporters

When pitching a story to a reporter or a writer, you need to be sure that you are pitching real news that will be interesting to their audience. Every writer or editor has a target audience and will write about specific topics. The best way to have a story covered is to build a relationship with writers and pitch to people whom you know. If you follow some simple rules, you are also more likely to have your story covered:

1. Research writers to learn what they like to write about
2. Only pitch to writers who cover stories like your story
3. Only pitch when you have real news, such as investment, a new corporate partnership, a product candidate in clinical trials or a product launch
4. Pitch with the problem you are solving and how you arc solving it
5. Tell a story
6. Use simple, clear language
7. Personalize your emails and have a catchy subject line
8. Write a compelling press release
9. Include photos and all other necessary company information in the media kit
10. Have a media contact who is available to speak with any reporters

Media Kit

It isn't easy to pitch to writers when you have never done it. Journalists and writers are busy people with short deadlines and little time to research stories. To help them out, and increase the likelihood of them writing about your story, you need to develop a media kit with all the information that they might need. There are several components to a media kit: the press release (also called a media release); contact details; images and company information *i.e.* company name, address, founding date and names of directors or management team.

The press release should be one page or less and lead with the key information: who, what, when, why and how. It is your elevator pitch wrapped inside your key news and shows writers why they should care. A press release states the problem and your solution and why you are different. Whenever you send a press release to a writer, ask yourself first whether that writer and their audience is even interested in this sort of news.

Here is a fictitious example of a press release:

Synthetic Stem Cells Could Eliminate Diabetes by 2030

SAN DIEGO, October 8, 2017 -- A new synthetic stem cell therapy from San Diego biotech company, Diabetes Solutions, has safely and effectively treated 35 patients with Type 1 Diabetes in a Phase I Clinical trial. The company is now in talks with several large pharmaceutical companies to bring this promising new treatment into the clinic.

Preliminary results from the Phase I trial show that 35 of the 50 patients who received three doses of DS001 had normal blood glucose and insulin levels within two months of the final dose. The remaining 15 patients produced some insulin, but not enough to control their blood glucose levels. This is the first time fully synthetic stem cells have been trialed in humans.

"We have built a synthetic pancreatic stem cell with the regenerative capacity of natural stem cells but without the ability to cause cancer," said Jack Smith, endocrinologist and CEO of Diabetes Solutions. "I have seen too many patients struggle against this disease. I had to try and find a better solution. This solution will let their bodies produce insulin and end their dependency on injected insulin."

DS001 solves two of the major problems with stem cell therapy: cancer formation and delivery. The synthetic DS001 stem cells are encased in a protective capsule to prevent them from being degraded by enzymes in the blood and to make sure they are delivered to the pancreas. Pancreatic biopsies from five of the treated patients showed that they had functioning beta cells.

"Those functioning beta cells could only have come from DS001 cells," said Jack Smith.

About Diabetes Solutions

Diabetes Solutions Inc. is a biotechnology company developing synthetic pancreatic cells to treat diseases including Diabetes mellitus. Diabetes Solutions' unique platform offers a new approach to treating pancreatic diseases. The company is headquartered in San Diego and was founded in 2015 based on work from Dr Jack Smith's laboratory at the University of California, San Diego.

Become a thought leader

You can also build credibility by becoming a **thought leader** or **key opinion leader** in your field. You do this by publishing blog posts, white papers and journal articles in your research area and by presenting at conferences and trade shows. You can also guest blog or pitch article ideas to media outlets and trade publications.

Marketing Basics

Marketing is all communication with actual and future customers. A marketing plan will help you to market like a scientist. It will make sure you have marketing goals and a detailed plan on how you will achieve those goals. It will outline both your **marketing strategy** and your **marketing tactics**.

A marketing strategy is a big picture statement about how you will use marketing to achieve your sales and business goals. If your business goal is to develop a cure for Type 1 Diabetes (T1D), then your marketing strategy may be to reach T1D patients and healthcare providers across the US (or Europe or Japan).

Tactics are the specific methods you will use to reach these target customers, such as create a twitter account and follow anyone who comes up under the search for 'diabetes' or attend the Annual Clinical Conference on Diabetes and talk to at least five healthcare providers about how they treat patients and what they would like to see in a new product.

Goal	Strategy	Tactics
Increase patient awareness	Increase social media presence	Start twitter account, tweet three times a day and follow 500 people who talk about Diabetes
		Start a Facebook page, post three times a week
		Start a LinkedIn group and invite all my contacts to join, post once a day
Increase physician awareness	Attend key conferences	Join the American Diabetes Association
		Attend the Annual Clinical Conference on Diabetes, May 24-27, 2018
		Submit an abstract to the American Diabetes Association 78th Scientific Sessions, June 22-26, 2018

Marketing channels

Marketing channels, also known as **distribution channels**, are the ways in which you make a product or service available to customers. These can be direct or indirect. **Direct marketing** sells straight to customers, for example email marketing and social media marketing. **Indirect marketing** sells through wholesalers or distributers, for example small antibody manufacturers may sell their products to a large life science company like Thermo Fisher rather than trying to sell directly to consumers.

B2B or B2C

Before you can write a marketing plan, you need to know whether your customers are individual people or companies. If your customers are individual people, you are selling Business-to-Consumer (B2C). If your customers are companies, you are selling Business-to-Business (B2B). These different customers require different marketing strategies and tactics.

B2B or B2C?

You may start out as a B2C company and decide your product or service is better suited to a B2B sales and marketing model, or vice versa. This happened to Pierre-Mikael Legris, CEO of health data management company, Pryv. Pryv started with a B2C model. Their vision was to create tools to help patients manage their health data. However, they realized this wouldn't work and so pivoted to a B2B model. Pryv now has tools to help entrepreneurs securely store and manage any health data they use to build their products or services. Use and storage of health data is strictly regulated in the US, Europe and many other countries around the world.

In the B2B sales model, your customers' purchasing decision does not involve emotion. It is a logical decision based on economics. For example, a hospital or a payer wants to know that your product will be more cost-effective than what they currently use. Your messaging should show how your product outperforms competitors in terms of time and cost savings and/or improved performance and reliability. You can use marketing materials like white papers, feature comparisons, brochures, data sheets, case studies and technology guides.

In the B2C model, consumers make more emotional buying decisions. Patients want a new drug because they want to feel healthier and suffer from less side effects. They want to know how your solution will affect their lives and their health. Physicians want products that will lead to better outcomes for their patients. You can use marketing materials like patient or customer testimonials, videos and feature comparisons when marketing straight to consumers.

Sales funnel

Your ultimate goal with marketing is to increase revenue. Therefore, you need to target different marketing materials to different people, depending on how close they are to buying your product. This is called the **sales funnel** or **buying cycle.** There is no point educating someone on the problem if they are ready to buy. There is also no point showing how your product is better than competitors if the person has no idea what problem your product solves. You should design your website, blog posts and other marketing material with the stages of the sales funnel in mind.

Figure 12.1 outlines the stages in a sales funnel or buying cycle: being unaware of the problem; knowing about the problem; looking for solutions; comparing options and deciding to buy.

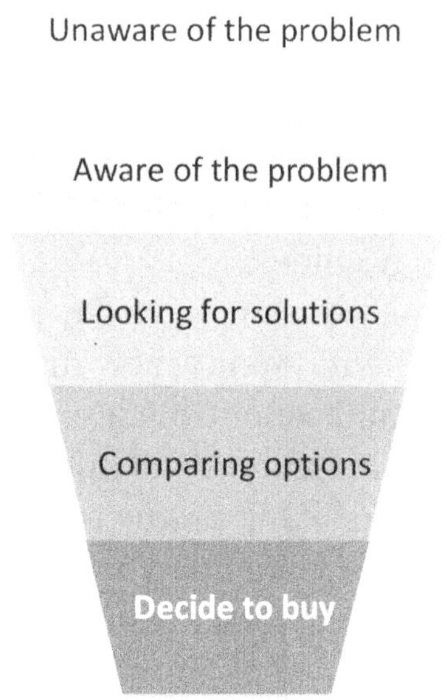

Figure 12.1 Sales funnel

By understanding where a customer is in the sales funnel, you can target your marketing message to advance them to the next stage, hopefully all the way to buying your product. A good way to do this is to have useful information on your website and to link the pages of your website in a logical way. That way, if someone searches for 'multiple sclerosis treatment options', you aren't taking them to a page that explains what multiple sclerosis is but rather to a page outlining how your new product candidate is better than current treatment options.

Buying cycles can be 12 months or longer for life science products. Many labs will only buy expensive equipment every few years. In contrast, patients may need a constant supply of a particular pharmaceutical. To effectively market your product to your target customers, you need to understand their buying cycle—how long it is, what the steps are and how to give the right information to the right people at each step. A key part of this is knowing who is making the buying decision in each organization (a purchasing officer, a researcher, a doctor), where their budget is coming from and when during the year their funds are available. This varies across organizations.

Goals *vs* Metrics

Your **marketing goals** are specific milestones that you want to achieve by a particular date. They should be well-defined, realistic, measureable and support your business goals. That means that each marketing goal should increase your sales or customers. You can increase or adapt your goals as you achieve them. Example goals are:

- Increase website traffic to 1,000 unique visitors per month
- Add 10 people each month to our email list
- Speak with five rheumatologists a month about our product

Metrics or **key performance indicators** (KPIs) will allow you to measure the progress of your product development and marketing plans. There are so many different metrics that you could measure and you can waste a lot of time measuring metrics that don't mean anything.

In his book 'The Lean Startup', serial entrepreneur and startup consultant Eric Ries discusses the importance of using actionable metrics instead of vanity metrics to measure your company growth. Vanity metrics are numbers that may look good but are not tied to growth or revenue. For example, you may see a 50% month-to-month increase in web traffic but if that doesn't convert to an increase in sales or investor enquiries, then it doesn't mean anything.

Actionable metrics relate to the number of customers who buy your product or use your service. They are things like **conversion rate** (the number of potential customers who start buying your product or service instead of a competitor's product or service) and **burn rate** or **drop-out rate** (the number of customers who stop using your product or service).

If people stop using your product or service, you should also them why through automated surveys or personal follow-up interviews. This information will help you tailor future marketing campaigns and product design.

For an early-stage life science company, it may take years to develop your lead product. Therefore, you won't be able to measure things like conversion rate and burn rate. However, you can do things like start an email newsletter and gather the names and emails of potential customers. The number of people on your email list is an actionable metric.

Measuring metrics

You need to repeatedly measure the same metrics to know whether your marketing strategies and tactics are working.

Google Analytics is a free tool that monitors website traffic and allows you to analyze your audience characteristics and behavior. You can see which pages draw people to your website, the **landing pages**, and how long they stay on your website.

You can keep track of social media followers in a spreadsheet. You can also keep track of any media mentions in a spreadsheet. It helps to add links on your website of any articles that mention your company and to download copies so you can easily keep track of your brand profile.

Email marketing automation platforms like MailChimp will help you collect and maintain an email list and send out email newsletters.

Partnerships

Marketing partnerships can be one of the best ways to reach more potential customers, especially for small companies with limited marketing budgets and expertise. Many life science startups will enter into development partnerships with large pharmaceutical companies to push their lead product candidates through preclinical and clinical development. These partnerships usually also include the larger company marketing the product.

You can still develop marketing partnerships even if you aren't in a position to enter into development partnerships. For example, if you are developing a reagent for a particular test or piece or equipment, you could co-market with the company that sells that test or reagent.

Referrals

Independent referrals are one of the most powerful forms of marketing. People are much more likely to believe what their friends, families and acquaintances tell them than what a stranger tells them. Therefore, it can really help your company if you start building your network early and cultivate contacts who could refer your company or products to other people.

Regulatory and legal concerns

There are some standard legal concerns with collecting and using personal data, and contacting people via email or social media. You must make it clear how you collected their data and how you will use it, and you must abide by the CAN-SPAM Act, which basically says that you cannot send spam email to people. Many organizations will block unsolicited emails and will black list you for trying.

Life science companies also have to navigate regulatory and legal guidelines that specify how you can use patient data (more on this in Chapter Four) and how and when you can market a healthcare product. You must abide by all regulations in all countries in which you wish to sell your products and obey these rules across all your media channels, including social media. For example, you cannot claim to have a product if your product has not been approved by the appropriate regulatory bodies.

Lastly, marketing and PR is all about building trust. False claims on any of your marketing material will undermine that trust. If you aren't first-in-class, don't say you are. If your test isn't 10-times faster than all competitors, don't say it is. Scientists analyze data for a living. Your potential customers will soon find out you embellished the truth and this news will spread quickly, especially across social media.

Budget

Marketing plans cost both time and money. You need to have a good idea where both these resources will come from. Set out your marketing goals and strategies and the specific tactics you will use to attain your goals. Then work out how much it will cost in terms of time and money. For example, it is free to set up most social media accounts but it will cost time to regularly post and interact with an audience through those channels. Likewise, if you have someone who likes to write on your team, it will cost very little money to set up a website and blog but that person may have to dedicate 10 hours a week to the task. If you don't have a writer on your team, you may have to outsource that work which will cost significantly more money. Good freelance writers can cost $50 to $100 an hour or more.

Creating a marketing budget will help you prioritize tactics so that you aren't trying to do too much at once.

Who will do the work?

Part of your budgeting is deciding who will do the work. Will you do everything in-house? Will current team members do the work or will you hiring a marketing expert to join your team (maybe in exchange for equity if you have no cash to pay salaries)? Or will you outsource the work by hiring consultants or full service agencies? Will you outsource small defined projects or your entire marketing plan?

Content marketing

Content marketing is the process of providing valuable content to make potential customers aware of your company and your product/s or service/s. It is based on the marketing concept of **reciprocity**—if you give someone something for free, they feel indebted to you and are more likely to do something for you in return, such as buy your product or tell relevant people about you.

To take advantage of reciprocity, you should add a **call to action** at the end of every piece of content you create. This is where you tell the reader what it is that you want them to do, for example, sign up to an email list or click through to another webpage to learn more about your product. A great example of this is the MailChimp website. MailChimp is an email marketing automation platform. You can join for free and send emails to up to 2,000 people. The homepage on the MailChimp website is very simple. It has the tagline 'Build your brand. Sell more stuff.' Underneath the tagline, in the middle of the page is a signup button that says 'Sign Up Free'.

For your calls to action to work, they need to be simple, clear and prominent. Also, the content you provide must be genuinely valuable to your target audience. For example, if you are developing a new diabetes treatment, you could create an email newsletter with news from many different sources about diabetes. In that newsletter, you could also include a link to a monthly article that you write on your company blog. This approach incorporates both email marketing and thought leadership.

It can take a year or longer to build an audience through a combination of content, social media and email marketing.

Basic content rules

There are basic rules to creating engaging content for life science audiences. These rules are the same whether you are creating a blog post, website or investor pitch deck.

- Tell a story
- Have a clear message
- Use simple language
- Show why you are different and better
- Show your expertise and establish trust
- Include a 'call to action'

- Obey legal and regulatory guidelines when describing your product candidates

Content types

To effectively market using content marketing, you need to segment your audience depending on their key problem and interests.

For potential investors and partners, you want to create content that shows the value of your technology and your product. This might include pages on your website, videos and graphics, blog posts, invited articles in established media outlets, white papers, academic papers and conference presentations.

For patients, you want to show how your product can improve their lives. This may be in the form of blog posts, social media posts, eBooks, articles, graphics, videos and webinars.

The key message and call to action for each audience segment will be different. The problems each segment faces will be different. Your goal with your content marketing is to solve the problems of each audience.

> ***Call to action***
>
> *A call to action is the next step that you want your target audience to take. If you want people who come to your website to sign up to your email list, put a 'sign up' button on your homepage and on the side of your other pages. If you want people to talk to their physician about using your product, give them a link to a downloadable brochure.*

Blogging

There are many advantages to blogging, both on your own website and on other websites. However, to reap any benefits from blogging, you should lay out a content plan for your blog and commit to regularly posting new articles.

Adding a blog to your website can help improve your rank in search engines by increasing your number of key words and by offering content that others will want to link to, thus helping increase the number of backlinks to your site. It can also be a useful content marketing tool where you establish your thought leadership and provide engaging content to keep your target audience interested.

Guest blogging is writing for other websites. While it can be hard to justify spending time writing for free for someone else, guest blogging can help you reach audiences that you couldn't otherwise reach. You can also include backlinks to your site in any guest blog posts that you write. Number of backlinks is one of the major parameters that search engines use to rank websites. The more backlinks you have, the higher you will rank. Guest blogging will also help you to become a recognized thought leader in your field.

Like all parts of your marketing plan, you can do this yourself or you can outsource it. If you don't like to write and don't have the budget to pay for professionals, you could contact local universities to see if they have a science writing program. Students in that program may be willing to write for you for free in order to gain experience. However, these students will not understand all the regulatory and legal considerations of life science marketing. Therefore, you will need to edit their work before publishing it on your site.

Social media

Billions of people spend hundreds of trillions of hours on social media platforms. For social media to work for you, you need to use the same platforms as your target audience and provide the content that they like to see. If you are developing a new arthritis treatment and most of your target customers are patients in their 60s or older, Twitter and Instagram may not be the best choice for you. However, if you are targeting rheumatologists who prescribe arthritis medication, you may find that some of these doctors are building their own brand and doing their own content marketing on Twitter or LinkedIn.

> ***Influencers***
>
> *Influencers are people who can influence the decisions of other people. Social media influencers are very active on their favorite platforms. If they like your company and your product, they can help you reach a larger audience by posting about you.*

Start with market analysis to work out who your target audiences are. Then research these audiences to understand which media outlets and social media platforms they use. Join these platforms and start to engage with **influencers**.

Email marketing

Email marketing can be a very powerful marketing tool. If you do collect and use any information from patients, even names and email addresses, you must abide by the data privacy guidelines in each country in which you operate. In the US, it is HIPAA and HITECH. In the EU, it is the General Data Protection Regulation (GDPR). I go through these regulations in more detail in Chapter Four.

An email newsletter will help you build an audience of potential customers. If you take them along your product development journey by sharing non-confidential information and company milestones, they will be more likely to tell their healthcare providers and insurance companies that they want your product. You can also use an email list to conduct customer surveys and use this information when you are designing your product.

There are a number of email marketing platforms. Some are free and some charge a monthly subscription fee. MailChimp is one of the most popular email platforms and is free if you have 2,000 subscribers or less.

Digital marketing

Digital marketing refers to any marketing through digital channels including the web and mobile phones. The basic concepts of digital marketing include:

- Designing a website that leads potential customers through a sales/marketing funnel
- Tracking website visitors
- Optimizing your website to rank highly in search engines through SEO techniques (keywords and backlinks)
- Digital advertising campaigns including pay per click ads and paid promotion on social media
- Affiliate marketing (where companies pay commission to external websites for the traffic or sales that they refer)

Life Science Advertising

There are very specific guidelines on advertising and selling life science products and services, particularly pharmaceuticals and medical devices. Do not start an ad campaign without reading the guidelines from the regulatory body in your country or consulting with a regulatory affairs expert.

In-person marketing/PR

There is still a place for in-person marketing and PR. Particularly if you are developing expensive laboratory equipment, which has a long sales cycle and requires work to convert customers from existing solutions.

Trade shows and conferences can be a good place to reach a targeted audience such as the specialist physicians who are most likely to prescribe your drug candidate if it is approved.

Life science startup marketing plan

Your startup marketing plan is a blueprint that helps you understand who your potential customers are and how to reach them. This will allow you to budget enough time and money to successfully reach customers. Your founding team may be the only people who ever read the full marketing plan but potential investors will still want to see a basic marketing summary. They want to know that you have a plan to reach your customers, that you have the ability to execute your plan and that you understand the costs involved. The only way to get this information is to go through the process of writing a marketing plan.

> *Your marketing plan should be fluid and should evolve to meet your company's goals. Measure the results of each tactic you employ. Use this information to understand what is and isn't working and re-write your plan as necessary.*

Here is a blueprint for how to write a startup marketing plan.

Executive Summary

Just like with a business plan, you should begin a marketing plan with an executive summary. This may be the only part that other people ever read. Write this at the end after you have finished all other sections. Take the key points from other sections and summarize them here.

Market size, Marketing and Business Goals

Start the main section of your marketing plan with an overview of the market size and of your business and marketing goals. Explain how your marketing goals will help support your business goals.

The Problem: Customer profiles and their pain

Define each target audience *e.g.* investor, patient, physician and create a short customer persona for each target audience. These personas are built from the market research you have done by researching content consumption and buying patterns of your different customers as well as any customer interviews. Talking to customers is the best way to find out what they want. You can supplement this with market research data purchased as reports from research companies.

Outline the key problem or pain point felt by each customer. This leads into the next section where you explain your solution for this problem.

Your solution: Product description

Describe each of your products or services in terms of development stage, product development pipeline, unique selling points, pricing and distribution. Always relate this back to how your product solves the pain of your target customers.

Competitive analysis

Outline competitors and their products and list their strengths and weaknesses. This helps you to make sure your products are well-positioned, which means they are different and better than competing products and meet a true need. Include information about which customers use which competing products and why, and what they do and don't like about them. Also include a plan on how you will convert these customers to your product, that is your **conversion strategy.**

Marketing strategy

Your marketing strategy explains how your product/s meet a real market need and how you will communicate this benefit to your target audience/s. Your strategy is how you will tell people how you solve their pain.

Marketing tactics

For each marketing goal, outline the tactics you will use to achieve that goal including timeline and budget. Include information on the marketing materials and channels you will use. Explain how you will execute your plan - who will do the work and how.

Financial projections

If you have any sales history, you can include that here. If not then include your timeline and budget required to achieve each goal. If you have a product on the market, also include projected revenues and customer acquisitions that you expect to achieve if you execute your marketing plan.

Measure, revise and repeat

Make a list of metrics that you will repeatedly measure to track growth and to verify whether or not you have attained your goals. Decide on how you will measure and track these metrics. Decide on what you will do if you don't achieve your goals.

Regularly analyze your metrics and use these to decide which tactics are working and which aren't. Revise your marketing plan to do more of the things that work and less of the things that don't.

Further Resources

Free online resources where you can find more information about the concepts outlined in this chapter.

Arrowhead Pharmaceuticals: www.arrowheadpharma.com

BCC Research Global Markets for Diabetes Therapeutics and Diagnostics (an overview of the report is free): https://www.bccresearch.com/market-research/healthcare/diabetes-therapeutics-diagnostics-markets-report-hlc029e.html

European Pricing and Reimbursement of Medicinal Products: https://ec.europa.eu/growth/sectors/healthcare/competitiveness/products-pricing-reimbursement_en

European Union Intellectual Property Office Trademark Information: https://euipo.europa.eu/ohimportal/en

fiverr: https://www.fiverr.com/

HARO: https://www.helpareporter.com/

HIPAA for Professionals: https://www.hhs.gov/hipaa/for-professionals/index.html

HIPAA Marketing Guidelines from the US Department of Health & Human Services: https://www.hhs.gov/hipaa/for-professionals/privacy/guidance/marketing/index.html

HITECH Act Enforcement Interim Final Rule: https://www.hhs.gov/hipaa/for-professionals/special-topics/HITECH-act-enforcement-interim-final-rule/index.html

Hubspot's 2017 Ultimate List of Marketing Statistics: https://www.hubspot.com/marketing-statistics

Six Degrees International Color Symbolism Chart: https://www.six-degrees.com/pdf/International-Color-Symbolism-Chart.pdf

Synthorx: www.synthorx.com

Upwork: https://www.upwork.com/

USPTO Trademark Database: https://www.uspto.gov/trademarks-application-process/search-trademark-database

Chapter Thirteen: Time Your Investor Pitch

Whenever I ask startup entrepreneurs about their biggest challenge, the answer is usually 'funding'. Building a life science company is expensive. The average cost of developing a new pharmaceutical is billions of dollars. Medical devices are much cheaper to develop, generally costing between $25 million and $100 million to get from idea to regulatory approval.

Most entrepreneurs don't have access to $25 million or more and so have no choice but to look for grant funding, private funding, loans and development partnerships to fund their product development pipeline.

At the beginning of a startup company's life, most entrepreneurs have limited funds. These funds might come from your own pocket or from friends and families or from a loan. These resources are finite and so you will likely have to choose between experiments because you can't afford to do everything. You probably won't be able to afford to work in a state-of-the-art lab. You may have to work on your startup while keeping a full-time or part-time job to support yourself financially. This lack of time and money means it takes longer to reach each milestone than you would like.

All this means that it is very tempting to chase external investment as soon as possible. With extra money, you could run the experiments you want to run and get to each milestone sooner, thus building a competitive advantage and getting closer to the all-important day when you bring in some revenue.

But there are some good reasons to hold out for as long as possible before you ask for private money. The more milestones you reach before asking for private investment, the more your company will be worth more and the less equity you will have to give up in exchange for the money. Also, investors are more likely to be interested in your company if you have already reached milestones such as having a working prototype or positive preclinical data. Lastly, many investors will want a seat on your board and will want to have a say in how you run your company. Entrepreneurs can benefit greatly from the network and wisdom of an investor who shares their vision for the company. On the flip side, it can be a great source of frustration if an investor does not agree with your ideas on how to develop your product/s and your business.

Investors are busy people who may see thousands of deals a year. Cold calls and emails from entrepreneurs usually go unanswered. Investors are most interested in companies referred by their trusted network. Tap into that network by building your own network of mentors and advisors. A good way to expand your network is to go to a demo day at an incubator or accelerator or participate in a business competition.

As a startup entrepreneur, you need to do as much as possible with as little money as possible. I have outlined ways to bootstrap and survive without investor funding in previous chapters. Take advantage of government grants and business competitions to find non-dilutive funding and get external validation of your science and your business model. Use community labs, incubators and accelerators to run your experiments as cheaply as possible. You can also consider partnering with research organizations or companies to do critical, early stage experiments. You might be able to work out an agreement to give development partners an equity stake or a share of future profits instead of paying cash. You can work from home instead of paying for an office. You might consider outsourcing experiments or hiring consultants and engineers from countries with cheap labor sources such as India or China.

If you have developed a unique platform or reagent or equipment, you may be able to perform contract research for clients as a way to bring in revenue and finance your product development.

Timing

When do you decide to ask for money? There is no easy answer to that question. It will depend on what sort of product you are developing. Medical devices, pharmaceuticals, wearables and medical software all have very different development timelines and costs. The more money you have, the faster you can develop your products or services. Without external funding, you run the risk of someone else developing and marketing a similar product before you do.

Ideally, you will pitch to investors after you have hit certain early milestones. An obvious time point would be when you are planning to do clinical trials as these are very expensive to run. However, depending on your financial situation and the product you are developing, you may not be able to get to the clinical trial stage without taking external investment. This is especially true if you are developing a novel drug candidate.

Advice on funding from Naresh Sunkara, former postdoc, now co-founder and CEO of Nosocom Solutions and founder of the Berkeley Postdoctoral Entrepreneur Program

1. *Look for government funding to at least get the proof of concept done.*
2. *Don't try to raise too much money. You will end up giving up too much of your company.*
3. *Be careful who you take money from. They need to bring value as well as bring money. I was recently offered funding of $200,000 in return for 45% of my company - I laughed at the offer.*
4. *Try not to waste money. Remember that most companies fail. Don't get a fancy office in the middle of downtown. After four years, I still have a home office.*

The first step when deciding when to ask for money and whom to ask, is to decide how much money you need and when you will need it. This means you need a detailed product development plan, including regulatory and marketing plans. You will need to break your plan down into steps and cost out each step. This will help you to understand how long it will take to get to the clinical trial stage and how much it will cost. Then you can plan where you will source that money from.

Investment Basics

If you are a first-time founder and you've never had to deal with fundraising, you are about to encounter a whole new world with its own set of rules and its own language. Here are some basic concepts and terms that you will need to know before you start talking to investors.

Exits

An **exit** in investment terms is when investors and/or founders take their money out of a company. This happens when a company is bought by a bigger company, as a **merger** or **acquisition**, or floats on a public stock exchange, through an **initial public offering** (IPO). The most common exit for life science startups is acquisition.

When you are pitching to investors, you need to have an exit strategy in mind. You need to know who is most likely to want to buy your company and how you will engage with potential acquirers.

Investors don't make any money until an exit occurs. All investors aim to have a 10x return on their investment. If they invest $500,000, they want to walk away with $5 million. The reason for this 10x goal is that 90% of startups fail, so investors can assume that 90% of their startup investments may fail. They look for a few big wins to cover the losses of other deals.

The difference between Angel and Venture Capital investors

Angel investors are high net-worth individuals who invest their own money. Venture capitalists (VCs) manage investment funds and invest other people's money. Historically this has meant that angels tend to invest less money in earlier, riskier funding rounds and VCs invest in larger, later rounds. However, this line is blurring with the rise of Super-Angel syndicates and Micro-VC firms.

> *The best way to understand how much any firm or group is likely to invest is to look at their previous investments or their portfolio. This will help you to understand the types of technologies and companies that interest each investor and work out who is most likely to want to put money into your company.*

Funding Rounds

Typically, a life science startup company will go through several funding rounds before an exit. With each round, you want to make sure you raise enough money to achieve your next major milestones. If you don't, it will be difficult to raise future rounds.

In each funding round, one of more investors will give you cash in exchange for equity, a convertible note or a simple agreement for future equity (safe).

Follow-on funding is when an investment firm that has already invested in your company chooses to invest in a subsequent round.

Seed Round

The seed round is the first round of funding for most startup companies, although you may have pre-seed money in the form of grants, loans, self-funding or friends and family investment. Companies that hit significant milestones before seeking private investment may skip their seed round and choose to go straight to raising a Series A funding round.

Seed rounds could be anywhere from $100,000 to over $1 million. According to the PwC MoneyTree Report, which collates data on all VC funding rounds in the US, the average venture-backed seed round in healthcare companies in 2016 was $1.4 million.

This money is typically used to build out your team and develop a working prototype or complete key preclinical studies.

Series A, B, C and beyond

After the seed round, the funding rounds are called Series A, B, C etc. Some life science companies raise a Series F or G round before they are acquired or go public. At each round, you are raising more money and your company needs to have a higher valuation to ensure that previous investors get an adequate return on their investment.

For all startups, Series A rounds are typically $1 million to $5 million, Series B are $6 million to $10 million and Series C and D can be $15 million to $50 million. However, in life science companies, the value of each round can be much higher. For example, Editas Medicine, which is commercializing CRISPR gene editing technology, raised a $43 million Series A round in 2013.

Series A rounds onwards are often funded by VCs, although Super-Angels may be involved. You will usually need to find several investors to meet your target for each funding round. A **lead investor** is the first investor to invest in a funding round and may help you find more investors to close out a round.

Convertible notes

You can receive investment in a straight exchange for equity, which you will give in the form of new shares issued during the investment round. However, more often than not, seed investors will prefer a **convertible note**, also called a convertible bond. This method is also frequently used for friends and family investments. When you raise investment as a convertible debt, the money you receive is considered a loan. Like any other loan, it has a principal amount, an interest rate and a maturity date. Unlike a standard loan, the principal amount plus any interest accrued will convert into equity at a future date, usually in a subsequent financing round. This means that investors are buying future shares in your company now. A convertible note delays the time when your shares are diluted.

The share price at which the debt will convert into equity will be set by your company valuation at the next funding round, unless you have a **cap** on your convertible note. If you have a cap, current investors will convert to equity at that capped amount per share even if your company shares have a higher value at the next funding round. For example, if you issue shares at $1.00 during the initial investment round with a cap of $2.00, then even if your shares are valued at $3.00 each in the next funding round, the original investors will only end up paying $2.00 per share.

The terms of the convertible note may also include a **discount** which will allow current investors to convert the debt owed into shares at a pre-determined discounted rate in a future funding round. These are both **anti-dilutive** measures that investors use to control how much their investment is diluted by future investment.

Safe

A simple agreement for future equity (safe) is similar to a convertible note but is not considered debt financing. Therefore, it does not include an interest rate and repayment requirement. This financial tool was created by Y Combinator, arguably the biggest startup accelerator in the world, and is now commonly used by the startups that go through the Y Combinator program.

Valuation

A **valuation** is what investors believe your company is worth or will be worth in the near future. A **pre-money valuation** is the value put on your company before you receive any investment or financing. Valuations of early stage life science companies are usually $5 million to $10 million or less.

*A **pre-money valuation** is the value of your company before an investment round. Pre-money valuations are used to calculate share price when issuing new shares in a funding round.*

*A **post-money valuation** is the value of your company after an investment round. Post-money valuations are higher because they include the value of the new investment money.*

If you are not making a profit - and most life science startups are not making money when they are pitching to investors - then you have to calculate the value of your company based on valuations of similar companies at the same stage and on your revenue and expense projections. Before you make any profit, the value of your company is hypothetical and reflects expectations of future value. Investors will take into account any **traction** you have made, *i.e.* whether you have sold any products or whether anyone is using your service, and will also look at your team's experience and **reputation**. This is where having an experienced co-founder can really help.

If you are taking in revenue, investors will look at the valuation of similar companies and the revenue they were making at that time. They then divide each company valuation by that company's revenue to calculate the

multiple. They will multiply this multiple by your revenue to come up with your valuation. This approach is much more common in tech startups than life science startups since product development is much slower and more expensive in life science.

Lawyers and accountants who have worked with many startups can help you decide on a ballpark valuation for your startup. You can use that figure as a starting place in negotiations with potential investors.

The valuation will dictate how much equity you will have to give up in return for funding. For example, if your company has a pre-money valuation of $2 million and you need $500,000 to run experiments over the next 18 months, investors will take 20% of your equity in exchange for that money. This is because your post-money valuation is equal to your pre-money valuation plus any new investment funding. Therefore, in this case, the post-money valuation will be $2.5 million. So, $500,000 will be worth 20% of the total company value. More about calculating share price in the 'Issuing shares' section below.

As a rule of thumb, you should ask for enough money to get you through the next 18 months or to the next major milestone. Investors want you to get to the next funding round or exit as quickly as possible because they do not see any return on their investment until you do.

However, you need to make sure that you are not giving up too much equity at this stage. You want the founders to still have over 50% of the equity, and thus have majority control, after Series A investment. This means that in a seed round, you only want to give up 25% or less of your equity.

The website Startups & Venture Capital has a good overview of nine different ways to calculate the pre-money value of your company (listed in the 'Further Resources' section).

Issuing shares

A share is a percentage ownership of a company with a nominal dollar value. Share value is calculated by dividing the value of the entire company by the number of shares that have been issued (these are called **outstanding shares**).

Share price = Company valuation/Number of outstanding shares

New shares are issued in each funding round. Investors 'buy' these shares with their investment money. When new shares are issued, this dilutes the value of existing shares because there are now more shares in the equity of the company.

For example, if your company's pre-money valuation (how much investors think your company is worth immediately prior to the new investment round) is $4 million and you have 2 million outstanding shares, then the share price is $4 million/2 million = $2.00.

If you are seeking new investment of $2 million, then your post-money valuation will be $4 million + $2 million = $6 million. Therefore, the new investment of $2 million will be worth 33% of the company ($2 million/$6 million = 33%)

Percentage ownership = Investment amount/total company value

Based on the share price of $2.00, the new investment of $2 million is worth 1 million shares. Since there were already 2 million outstanding shares before the investment and 1 million new shares will be issued in exchange for the new investment, there will now be 1 million + 2 million = 3 million outstanding shares. Therefore, all existing shareholders will have their share of the company diluted by the new shares.

Dilution and anti-dilution protection

The equity that each shareholder owns in a company is diluted with each funding round because new shares are issued. If we continue with the example above where the pre-money valuation was $4 million and there were 2 million outstanding shares, if the founders own 70% of those shares, they own 1.4 million shares before the new investment round.

With the new round, 1 million new shares were issued. So the founders' 1.4 million shares now make up 47% of the equity (1.4 million/(2 million + 1 million) = 47%).

Likewise, if existing shareholders owned 30% of the shares before the new investment round, they owned 600,000 shares. After the new investment round, their shares account for only 20% of the company.

Most investors will include some anti-dilution measures in any investment agreement to minimize the dilution that occurs with new investment rounds. An example of this is a cap on a convertible note, as discussed in the 'Convertible note' section earlier in this chapter.

As discussed in Chapter Eleven, most investors will want to be issued preferred shares. These shares come with certain rights, such as voting rights and the rights to be paid their share of any dividends or any proceeds from the sale of the company before common shareholders are paid.

The sale of your company is called a **liquidation event** because the company value is converted into cash at that point. A liquidation event is when investors get their investment back plus their share of any profit. In most cases, preferred shares will convert to common shares at any liquidation event.

Investors may include **anti-dilution provisions** in any investment agreement to re-calculate the rate at which their preferred shares convert to common shares. These provisions aim to make sure that early-stage investors can convert to common shares at a rate that compensates for the dilution they experienced by holding shares through multiple investment rounds.

More on anti-dilution provisions in the 'Term sheet' section of Chapter Fourteen.

Cap table

Every time you take investment or issue shares, you need to enter that transaction into your capitalization (cap) table. A cap table is a running list of shareholders, shares and financing rounds. You can find an example cap table at Venture Hacks, a startup advice website run by the founders of AngelList. It helps you keep track of who owns what and will also help you to project ownership dilution as you proceed through financing rounds and issue more shares. The more investors you have, the messier and more complicated your cap table becomes.

Investors don't like messy cap tables. This is something to keep in mind if you decide to raise money from friends and family or use crowd-funding or crowd-investing sites. You want to keep the number of investors to a minimum if possible. A good lawyer who has worked with startups can help you make sure that your corporate structure is sound and won't prevent you from getting private investment.

Whom to approach?

Investors are understandably wary of startup companies, particularly of life science startups. Nine out of ten startups fail. Less than 10% of Phase I clinical trial candidates are approved by the FDA.

It is important to choose investors who have the knowledge, expertise and network to help you build your company and find follow-on funding.

You don't have to go straight to angel or VC investors. There are many other sources of funding. I have already gone through grants and loans in Chapter Seven. Here is a list of potential investors you could ask to help fund your startup.

Friends and Family

Friends and family are an obvious choice when you are looking for money. It is easy to assume that you don't need to treat friends and family investment with the same rigor that you would an institutional investor. However, if you take investment from friends and family, you should still follow ethical and financial guidelines. This will help make sure you don't destroy valuable relationships and will also make it easier to take future investment. Investors like to see clean and well-documented financial records.

Also, any investment, including those by friends and family in US companies are subject to state and federal

> ***Accredited investors***
>
> *The guidelines on who can become an accredited investor vary from country to country but in general, you have to meet certain earning or asset thresholds to be accredited. In the US, you must have earned at least $200,000 each year for the past two years or have over $1 million in assets, excluding your primary residence.*

securities laws. These laws require that anyone who invests in your company is an accredited investor or is able to bear the economic risk of the investment. This means that you cannot legally take money from anyone who can't afford it, no matter how much they want to help you. You must also provide any investor with the information you would normally have in a prospectus. Lastly, securities law requires that anyone who invests in a private company agree to not resell or distribute their shares or equity.

Securities law in the US essentially prevents you from advertising or publicly soliciting for investors. If you ask a room full of non-accredited investors to invest in your private company, you are breaking the law. This is considered a 'public offering' and must be approved by the Securities and Exchange Commission (SEC).

If you want to set a share price when raising money from friends and family, you could issue common stocks in exchange for the investment.

If you don't want to set a price for your shares now, you could consider using a convertible note. With a convertible note, your friends and family have the right to convert the money they have loaned you into equity at a future date. Investors will calculate a valuation of your company, which will dictate share price, at the next funding round and any outstanding convertible notes will convert at this share price unless you include a cap and/or a discount in your convertible note.

Other options are to take money from friends and family as a standard loan that you will repay in cash instead of convert to equity. Don't draw up a 'no interest' loan as this can cause tax issues for lenders, particularly in the US. The Internal Revenue Service (IRS) will often apply the market rate to any 'no interest' loan values on personal tax returns and thus presume that your family and friend lenders are receiving the market interest rate from you in addition to any principal repayments.

If you do decide to take friends and family money as a loan, it will help if you draft flexible loan repayments to let you manage the cash flow in your startup.

Angel Investors

Angel investors are high net-worth individuals who invest their own money. Venture capitalists, in contrast, manage investment funds, and therefore, invest other people's money. Angels tend to invest in syndicates where ten or more individual angel investors will each invest a small amount of money *e.g.* $25,000 to $50,000. This means that when you have angel investment, you will likely need to report to many different investors. On one hand, this gives you the benefit of receiving advice from a range of people with a range of experience. On the other hand, it creates more work for you and it can be very time consuming to report to ten or more different people.

Angels, like VCs, will conduct background research on a company, called **due diligence**, before deciding whether or not to invest. Each angel will have a specific background and experience and may have personal preferences as to the type of company in which they will invest.

In 2016, the median angel investment in the US was $127,000. These investments were part of a median round size of $950,000. This means that most entrepreneurs had to find multiple investors to close a round. These include all the investor types listed in this chapter, not only angels and VCs.

US Angel Investors

In 2016, US angel groups invested $3.5 billion in 2,751 deals, 17% of which involved healthcare companies. Over 30% of these angel-backed deals were in California. Nearly half (49.6%) were new company deals and 50.4% were follow-on deals.

It helps if you approach investors close to where your company is based. The majority of angel-backed investments in 2016 were in companies in the same region as the investors. Depending on the region around the US, 58-93% of the angel investment deals were 'in region' in 2016.

That being said, investors will look further afield for the right opportunities. In 2016, US angel groups invested in companies in 20 different countries including Australia, Canada, China, India, Mexico and the UK.

Where to find US Angels

There are hundreds of angel investor groups and thousands of individual angel investors in the US. To find them, you can use online search tools at AngelList and the Angel Capital Association (ACA). AngelList lists individual investors, their country of residence, their industry focus and the number of investments they have made. The ACA has a comprehensive list of angel groups working across North America. They also publish the annual Halo report on angel investments in the US.

Life Science Angels

Life Science Angels (LSA) is one of the best-known healthcare focused angel groups. They are based in the Bay Area, California. Since 2005, they have invested over $50 million in 58 startups, 14 of which have exited. LSA portfolio companies have raised over $1 billion in subsequent funding.

Tech Coast Angels

Tech Coast Angels (TCA) is one of the most prolific angel groups in the US. They are based in California and have invested over $170 million in over 300 companies. These companies have gone on to attract over $1.6 billion in subsequent funding. TCA also runs an annual QuickPitch competition in conjunction with San Diego Venture Group.

Keiretsu Forum

Keiretsu Forum is another very active investment group. They are a global community of angels, VC and corporate investors with chapters in 16 countries including the US, Canada, the UK, France, Israel, China, India, Japan, South Korea and Australia. Keiretsu Forum invested in at least seven life science companies in 2017.

Others

Investors Circle, Golden Seeds, Central Texas Angel Network and Houston Angel Network are a few more of the most active American angel groups.

European Angel Investors

You can search for European angel investors at AngelList. Techstars also has a very useful digital map of active investors in Europe and the US.

Angel Investment Network is an online platform with a database of nearly 150,000 registered angels across the UK and the world. You can register as an entrepreneur on Angel Investment Network, add a pitch and connect with any interested investors.

The European Commission has launched Startup Europe, an initiative that aims to connect entrepreneurs with investors and advisors. You can join the Startup Europe Map to learn more about who is most active in which countries.

The UK Business Angels Association has an online member directory. You can search for investors by type (e.g. angel, VC, crowdfunding platform or incubator/accelerator), investment range, region and sector focus.

All these websites are listed in the 'Further Resources' section at the end of this chapter.

Venture Capitalists

Venture capitalists are professional investors who manage investment funds. VCs tend to fund larger investment rounds than angels and will usually conduct more in-depth due diligence than angel investors. They will often also require a seat on the board of a company as part of the investment terms. Angel investors usually do not ask for this.

VCs in the US invested $7.5 billion in healthcare companies in 2016 and this is likely to be higher in 2017, according to the Silicon Valley Bank 2017 report.

In 2016, European healthcare companies raised €1.8 billion from VCs in 330 rounds. Almost 25% of this money went to companies in London and 23% went to companies in Paris.

VCs are professionals who may screen through thousands of companies a year. Less than 1% of startups secure VC funding. You can increase your chances of success by polishing your pitch and your business documents and by targeting VCs who have invested in similar companies to your startup. You have a much better chance of hearing back from a VC if you can organize a warm introduction from someone in your network. As Bruce Booth, partner at Atlas Venture, writes on his blog Life Sci VC, cold emails and calls have “a hit rate near zero”.

Look for specific partners within VC firms who have sponsored deals with companies like your company - the same stage of funding, size of company and type of technology. And make sure this partner is not on the board of ten or more companies right now. If they are, they will have very little time to help you. Also look for VC firms that have raised a new fund within the last four years, ideally dedicated to life science. These firms are actively looking to invest.

Studies of VC investment patterns show they have several biases. Being aware of these can help you craft your pitch. Half of all VC investments in the US between the years of 1980 and 2009 were in companies headquartered within 233 miles of the VC office, so it helps to approach local offices. VCs also have a similarity bias. They prefer to invest in entrepreneurs who have some similarity to themselves - have gone to the same university, come from the same town or have worked in the same company. VCs also use past investing experience to decide on future investments.

Top Life Science VCs in the US

Here are some of the most active and prestigious VCs in the US that invest in life science companies. Investments from these VCs come with the added benefits of access to the expertise and networks of seasoned industry professionals.

New Enterprise Associates

New Enterprise Associates is a global investment firm with over $20 billion in 16 investment funds. They invest in technology and healthcare, including biopharma, medical device and healthIT companies.

OrbiMed

OrbiMed is a healthcare investment fund that has been operating for over 20 years and currently manages $13 billion investment in companies across the world. They focus on life science companies.

Third Rock Ventures

Third Rock Ventures invests in biotech and healthcare companies. They manage $1.9 billion across four funds. They are known for funding 'riskier' companies than other VC firms. A number of their portfolio companies are now public, including Editas Medicine, Bluebird Bio and Sage Therapeutics.

Kleiner, Perkins, Caulfield and Byers

Kleiner, Perkins, Caulfield and Byers has $10 billion across 20 venture funds and has invested in over 850 companies. They invest in both tech and biotech companies.

First Round Capital

First Round Capital only invests in the first funding round for each company. They invest across a range of industries including healthcare. They only invest in companies located in North America, usually in the US.

Sequoia

Sequoia is a VC firm that has been operating since 1972. Companies in which Sequoia has invested are now worth over $1.4 trillion. While Sequoia invests across a range of industries, they have backed many successful life science companies.

Atlas Venture

Atlas Venture is a VC firm in Cambridge, Massachusetts that only invests in life science companies. They have invested in over 150 companies since 1990. Atlas raised a $350 million fund in 2017 to invest in early-stage life science companies. Bruce Booth, a partner at Atlas, writes the Life Sci VC blog, which is syndicated by Forbes, and provides insider advice on pitching to venture capital investors.

Flagship Pioneering

Flagship Pioneering (previously Flagship Ventures) was founded in 2000 and is based in Cambridge, Massachusetts. They have invested in 75 companies that are now worth over $19 billion. Flagship companies, including Moderna Therapeutics and Seres Therapeutics, collectively own more than 500 patents and have conducted more than 50 clinical trials. Flagship funds early stage companies that develop high impact technologies to address serious health and sustainability issues.

SV Health Investors

SV Health Investors (previously SV Life Sciences) is a life science and healthcare VC firm based in Boston and San Francisco in US and in London in the UK, with over $2 billion under management. They are interested in biotech, medical device, digital health and healthcare service companies.

Top European Life Science VCs

Here are some of the biggest European VC firms that invest in life science companies. You can find more on the labbiotech.eu website.

Woodford

Woodford is a British investment firm with a €1.1 billion fund dedicated to investing in life science companies.

Abingworth

Abingworth is a life science and healthcare investment fund based in the UK, with an office in Boston, Massachusetts in the US. Since 1973, they have raised $1.9 billion across 11 life science funds. Abingworth has invested in 143 life science companies that have had 64 IPOs and 44 M&A exits.

Index Ventures

Index Ventures was founded in 1996 in Geneva, Switzerland and now has offices in London in the UK and San Francisco in the US. They have invested in 160 tech and healthcare companies in 24 countries, although healthcare is only a small part of their portfolio.

Medicxi

Medicxi is an independent investment firm based in London that was spun out from Index Ventures. They launched in 2016 with two funds, one for early-stage companies and a $300 million late-stage fund. They have invested in at least 10 life science companies at the seed stage and 36 later stage companies.

Life Science Partners (LSP)

Life Science Partners is a life science-focused investment firm based in Amsterdam, Munich and Boston. LSP has raised over €1.1 billion in funds and invested in over 100 companies.

Sofinnova Ventures

Sofinnova is a venture capital firm that has focused exclusively on life sciences since 2007. They manage $2.2 billion of funds and invest in clinical-stage biopharmaceutical companies.

Reward or Donation Crowdfunding

If you don't yet need large amounts of money, or are trying to bootstrap to meet a milestone before looking for investment, you could try to raise funds through crowdfunding. There are two types of crowdfunding.

The first is reward or donation crowdfunding where people give money as a donation or they purchase a product or service that has not yet been developed. Most people raise only small amounts of money in the range of $1,000 to $10,000 through these sites.

The second is equity or debt crowdfunding where companies raise money from many different investors in return for equity or as a loan. I'll talk about equity and debt crowdfunding in the next section.

Kickstarter

Kickstarter is one of the best-known reward crowdfunding sites. Since 2009, Kickstarter has funded 130,829 projects.

Over 13 million people have given a total of $3.3 billion on the site in exchange for rewards or products or services that are yet to be developed. Very few projects on Kickstarter are science-based.

Experiment

Experiment is a science-focused reward crowdfunding site. The Experiment team reviews all projects before listing them on the site. Thousands of scientists have used the platform to raise small amounts of money. However, scientists must share the results of any experiments funded through Experiment with their backers. Before using Experiment, you should make sure that this won't compromise any IP protection strategies.

Thinkable

Thinkable is a reverse crowdfunding site. The platform allows universities, philanthropic groups and other organizations to hold scientific competitions. Scientists can register for a competition and post their eligible project. This gives them the chance to win cash prizes but also provides a platform to promote their work and allows them to connect with potential funders. Using the Thinkable platform, or any crowdfunding platform, is a form of publication and will count as prior art. Do not post any IP that you haven't yet patented on a crowdfunding site.

Equity or Debt Crowdfunding and Investor Websites

In equity or debt crowdfunding, a 'crowd' of investors invests in a startup in exchange for either equity or debt. This is not a donation or a purchase of future goods like the crowdfunding models of sites such as Kickstarter.

Dozens of equity and debt crowdfunding sites have launched in the last five years. They all have different terms. Some allow only **accredited investors** to invest in the companies listed on their platform. Others allow anyone to invest small amounts up to a certain percentage of their income. Some platforms count each investor individually, meaning you will end up with many shareholders in your cap table. Others bundle everyone who invested through their platform into one 'investor' to simplify the investment round.

Each equity or debt crowdfunding site screens applications and only allows startups that meet certain criteria to fundraise through their platform. These criteria are generally the same things that angels and VCs look for in life science startups:

- You have a **novel technology** that is protected by patents
- Your technology can be developed into one or more **products** that address a **true market need**
- You have a **large addressable market**
- Your team is **capable of executing** on your product development and business plan

You should investigate each platform thoroughly and ideally speak to other entrepreneurs who have used the sites before deciding which platform is best for you.

Here are some of the biggest equity and debt crowdfunding sites.

SeedInvest

SeedInvest allows startups to raise funding in exchange for equity from VCs, angels and crowd investors. Anyone can join SeedInvest as an individual non-accredited investor, what I call 'crowd investors'. SeedInvest co-invests $200,000 in every fundraising deal on its site. There are over 180,000 investors in the SeedInvest community and more than 240 companies have used the platform to raise an average of $500,000.

Propel(x)

Propel(x) is an investor marketplace that only lists tech and science startups. Only accredited investors can invest through the site.

AngelMD

AngelMD is an online investment platform for medical startups including medical device and digital health companies. Only accredited investors can invest through the site.

Republic

Anyone 18 years or older can invest amounts from $10 in startups listed on the Republic platform. Companies must be incorporated in the US to use the site. Startups can raise money from angel groups alongside individual non-accredited investors. Republic bundles crowd investors together to make it easy and simple for startups to take investment from many people.

OurCrowd

OurCrowd is an equity crowdfunding platform co-founded in 2013 by the Israeli venture capitalist John Medved. The platform has 20,000 accredited investors from 112 countries and has raised $450 million for 120 companies. Only accredited investors may invest through OurCrowd.

In each funding round, VCs, angel groups or large biotech and pharma companies co-invest with individual investors. 15 **medtech** (medical device and diagnostic) companies have raised between $1 million and $6 million through OurCrowd.

The team behind OurCrowd have also launched Radicle, a VC fund focused on agricultural technologies (**AgTech**) and Qure, a digital health investment fund.

Off3r

Off3r is an aggregator of online investment sites, including equity crowdfunding sites. It is European-focused but does list startups from other regions around the world. The companies come from many different industries. You can search through thousands of investment opportunities (*i.e.* startups) and filter search results by industry, platform on which the startup is listed or location (UK, Europe or the rest of the world).

This is a great site to use to understand which platforms list which sorts of startups and which startups are most successful at raising money through equity crowdfunding sites. Off3r links through to 12 different equity crowdfunding platforms including Invesdor, CrowdForAngels and Angels Den.

Invesdor

Invesdor links startups in the UK and Scandinavia (Denmark, Finland, Norway and Sweden) with crowd investors around the world. They currently have over 50,000 investors, 206 companies listed and have had 96 successful funding rounds with €36 million invested. Startups can choose to raise money through Invesdor as either an equity offering or a bond offering. Anyone can invest using this platform.

> ***Crowdfunding tips from Julie Legault, designer and founder and CEO of Amino Labs***
>
> *Be very aware of the actual costs. Times your gut feeling cost by 2.5 and then you might break even. Our BOM back when we crowdfunded was so very unrealistic. But we wanted to get out there, and we've been using some of the funding we got from IndieBio to cover costs, and now a portion of our current sales also goes back to covering that campaign.*
>
> *Mistakes were made!*

Family Offices

Family offices manage money for wealthy families. There are more than 3,000 of these offices around the world, managing $4 trillion. They can be either single-family offices (SFOs) or multi-family offices (MFOs). All family offices aim to maintain and increase the wealth of their family or families. Each office and family will have their own investment strategy and biases and unlike VCs, this information is not public and can be difficult to find. Families want to stay anonymous and keep their financial details as private as possible. Entrepreneurs need to tap into their network of advisors, mentors and investors to get to know which family offices might be interested in funding their company.

If you don't have any mentors or advisors who can help you find the right family office, you could turn to brokers or capital raisers. These are people whose job is to fundraise. They may be able to help you get in touch with family offices or other investors in exchange for a percentage of the funding that you raise. Brokers will not introduce you unless they are impressed with your company, team and investment pitch. They must believe that investors are likely to invest in you before they will introduce you. However, investors generally prefer companies referred by their trusted network than by brokers.

Like VCs, family offices provide mentorship and connections as well as funding and will likely require a seat on the board of any companies in which they invest. However, they may offer more flexible investment terms and timelines than VCs.

Patient Advocacy Groups

There are thousands of patient advocacy and support groups around the world. Many of these organizations provide medical research grants. The total grant money offered by patient advocacy groups is more than $500 million each year.

Many of these groups also partner with life science companies to support the development of new diagnostics and treatments for their disease of interest. This investment approach is called **venture philanthropy**. Patient advocacy groups offer financial support of drug or device development programs in exchange for equity or a share in the royalties.

A notable example of venture philanthropy is the Cystic Fibrosis Foundation's partnership with Vertex Pharmaceuticals to support Vertex's development of two drugs to treat cystic fibrosis: Kalydeco® (ivacaftor) and Orkambi® (ivacaftor/lumacaftor). Vertex made over $1 billion from the sale of those two drugs in 2015. The Cystic Fibrosis Foundation has also made a lot of money from those two drugs. They sold their royalty rights to Kalydeco and Orkambi in 2014 for $3.3 billion.

The Cystic Fibrosis Foundation has invested over $425 million in drug development pipelines in a number of biotech and big pharma companies. They have helped fund almost every cystic fibrosis drug on the market.

The Michael J. Fox Foundation has also invested millions of dollars in biotech and pharma companies developing treatments for Parkinson's Disease.

Unlike angels, VCs and family offices, whose goal is to make money, the goal of patient advocacy groups is to find new treatments and cures for specific diseases.

The World Health Organization has a list of patient support groups. This list can help you find groups that might be interested in partnering with your company. You can find similar lists on the National Health Council and National Institutes of Health websites.

Philanthropic Organizations

Philanthropic organizations that are not linked to a single disease type also invest in life science companies. In 2015, the Bill and Melinda Gates Foundation, the largest philanthropic organization in the world, invested $52 million in CureVac, a German biotech company. They have invested, or given grants, to over 20 biotech and pharma companies including Moderna Therapeutics and pharma giant Takeda Pharmaceuticals.

The Wellcome Trust is a medical charity in the UK. They formed an independent subsidiary called Syncona in 2012. Syncona has £250 million in investment funds to invest in companies that focus on unmet medical needs.

Like with patient advocacy groups, these philanthropic investments have the over-riding goal of improving life for patients around the world rather than making money.

Co-development partnerships

Larger biotech and pharma companies will often enter into **joint development partnerships** with smaller companies to develop a drug candidate or platform. Companies such as Pfizer have an entire department dedicated to fostering partnerships and list their partnership areas of interest on their websites. Over 50% of Genentech's marketed and pipeline products are from partnerships.

The terms of each partnership will vary but usually include the resources that each company will dedicate to the project and the milestones that each company is expected to meet. The larger company will give cash to the smaller company either as an upfront payment or on completion of milestones, or both, in exchange for equity, partial or complete ownership of the product under development or a share in royalties.

> *Make sure you understand all the agreement details before you sign a joint development partnership. Partners may ask for preferential rights such as the right to acquire at a specific price. This may spook future investors.*

As well as the benefit of cash, these partnerships allow smaller companies to benefit from the product development, manufacturing and marketing expertise of the larger company.

Further Resources

Free online resources where you can find more information about the concepts outlined in this chapter.

Abingworth: http://www.abingworth.com

Accredited Investors (US Securities and Exchange Commission): https://www.sec.gov/fast-answers/answers-accredhtm.html

Angel Capital Association: https://www.angelcapitalassociation.org/

Angel Investment Network (UK): https://www.angelinvestmentnetwork.co.uk/

Angel Resource Institute Halo Report 2016: https://angelresourceinstitute.org/media/upload/full-report-2016haloreport.pdf

AngelMD: https://www.angelmd.co/

Atlas Venture: https://atlasventure.com

Central Texas Angel Network: http://centraltexasangelnetwork.com/

Classes of shares: http://www.companylawclub.co.uk/classes-of-shares

Company House (UK): https://www.gov.uk/government/organisations/companies-house

Dealroom.co 2016 European Venture Capital Report: https://blog.dealroom.co/wp-content/uploads/2017/01/2016-European-Venture-Capital-Report.pdf

Experiment: https://experiment.com

First Round Capital: http://firstround.com

Flagship Pioneering: http://flagshippioneering.com/

Golden Seeds: http://www.goldenseeds.com/

Houston Angel Network: http://houstonangelnetwork.org/

Incorporation and names – Guidance from the UK Government: https://www.gov.uk/government/publications/incorporation-and-names/incorporation-and-names

Index Ventures: https://www.indexventures.com

Internal Revenue Service Business Structures: https://www.irs.gov/businesses/small-businesses-self-employed/business-structures

Invesdor: https://www.invesdor.com/en

Investors' Circle: http://investorscircle.net/

Keiretsu Forum: http://www.keiretsuforum.com/

Kickstarter: https://www.kickstarter.com

Kleiner, Perkins, Caulfield and Byers: http://kpcb.com

Medicxi: https://medicxiventures.com

Legal Tips for Startups: http://lifesciencenetwork.com/blogs/lsn-editorial-team/2017/03/06/legal-tips-for-startups

Life Science Angels: https://lifescienceangels.com/

Life Science Partners (LSP) Amsterdam https://lspvc.com

Life Sci VC: https://lifescivc.com

New Enterprise Associates: http://www.nea.com/

Off3r: https://www.off3r.com/compare/Equity-Crowdfunding

Orbimed: http://www.orbimed.com/

OurCrowd: https://wwwng.ourcrowd.com

Propel(x): https://www.propelx.com/

PwC MoneyTree Report: https://www.pwc.com/us/en/technology/moneytree.html

Republic: https://republic.co

SeedInvest: https://www.seedinvest.com

Set Up a Private Limited Company (UK): https://www.gov.uk/limited-company-formation

Setting Up a Limited Company: How to Issue Shares (UK): https://startups.co.uk/setting-up-a-limited-company-how-to-issue-shares/

Sequoia: https://sequoiacap.com

Sofinnova Ventures: www.sofinnova.com

Startup Europe: http://startupeuropeclub.eu/about-us/

Startup Europe Map: http://www.startupeuropemap.eu/

Startups and Venture Capital: Valuation for Startups – 9 Methods Explained: https://startupsventurecapital.com/valuation-for-startups-9-methods-explained-53771c86590e

SV Health Investors: http://svhealthinvestors.com/

Tech Coast Angels: https://www.techcoastangels.com/

The Entrepreneur's Guide to a Biotech Startup, Fourth Edition: https://ctsi.ucla.edu/researcher-resources/files/view/docs/EGBS4_Kolchinsky.pdf

Thinkable: https://thinkable.org

Third Rock Ventures: http://thirdrockventures.com

The 10 Key Legal Documents for Your Business: https://www.entrepreneur.com/article/236967

UK Business Angels Association Member Directory: https://www.ukbaa.org.uk/services-for-entrepreneurs/contact-investors/search-the-ukbaa-database/

Venture Hacks Cap Table: http://venturehacks.com/articles/cap-table

Venture Beat: Family Money: https://venturebeat.com/2017/03/25/family-money-an-emerging-funding-source-for-startups/

What is Weighted Average Anti-Dilution Protection: http://www.startupcompanylawyer.com/2007/08/04/what-is-weighted-average-anti-dilution-protection/

World Health Organization: Patient Support Groups: www.who.int/genomics/public/patientsupport/en/

Woodford: https://woodfordfunds.com

Chapter Fourteen: Pitch Like a Pro

Your exact pitch will depend on the people to whom you are pitching. No matter whom you are pitching, you must align your goals with their mission. Each individual investor will have a different mission. Do your background research to try and understand what that mission is. Know your audience and their motivations. Your job when pitching is to make the investor, or potential partner, want to know more about you and your company.

> *"One of the first things people would ask me when I pitched my idea is, 'What do you know about this problem and why are you the right person to address this?'"*
>
> ***Guillermo Vela, former scientist, now CEO and co-founder of Nebulab***

Only pitch investors who are interested in companies like your company. There is no point approaching a VC who only invests in tech companies if you are developing a drug candidate to treat heart disease, or applying for an SBIR grant from the National Cancer Institute when you are developing a novel malaria vaccine technology. It takes a lot of time to write a grant application or create a pitch deck and business plan. You want to invest your time wisely by only targeting investors and funders who are interested in your technology.

This is a two-way street. It is just as important for the health and future of your company that investors are aligned with your mission. Otherwise you may find them pulling your company in directions that you do not want to go.

Despite their individual differences, all investors, no matter who they are, want to know these things about any startup:

- you are **different**
- you **own novel technology** and are developing it into a **unique product** that solves a **real need** for a **big market** (or their target market, in the case of patient advocacy groups *i.e.* you have an excellent **product-market fit**)
- you have a plan to create and market your product/s or service/s
- you have the **capability to execute** your plan
- you **need the investor's money** to execute your plan (including how you will spend that money)
- now is the **right time** to make your product
- you are **passionate** and truly believe in what you are doing and will work non-stop until you achieve your goals

Your entire pitch and all supporting documents must articulate these points. This holds true whether you are applying for a grant through a patient advocacy group or a government organization, speaking to a family office or pitching to a room full of angels and VCs.

Some investors see hundreds or thousands of deals a year and only invest in one. You have to be better than *everyone else* to get their money.

Value proposition

Your **value proposition** is your unique selling point. It is a short statement that explains why a customer should buy your product or use your service. A value prop should include the problem you are addressing, your solution and why you are better than competitors. Another term used to describe this is **killer app**. Your killer app is the core value of your technology that makes you better than competitors and attractive to customers.

Elevator pitch

An elevator pitch is a succinct description of your company that you can give in about 30 seconds. This is very difficult to perfect because in that short time you need to explain what you are doing, why, why you love it, and any **traction** you have achieved. Your goal is to get the person listening interested enough to ask more questions.

You never know when you might meet an investor or mentor or potential new team member so you should always have an elevator pitch ready and should always be refining it based on feedback from everyone who has heard it.

> ***Startup Traction***
>
> *In the words of Naval Ravikant, CEO and co-founder of AngelList, startup traction means "quantitative evidence of market demand". It means showing that customers want your product or service.*

Pitching tips

Any pitch is a form of science communication, whether it is an elevator pitch, a grant application, or a full investor pitch with a slide deck. If you follow some simple rules you are more likely to successfully communicate your message.

You have two minutes to make a first impression and in most situations, people judge you more on your non-verbal than verbal communication. This means that body language and how you deliver your words are just as important, if not more important, than your actual words.

Your goal with any pitch is to get another meeting with the investors.

Practice

Practice your pitch hundreds of times. Then keep practicing. Practice in front of the mirror. Present to family and friends. Video yourself. You may cringe but it will show you where you need to improve. Do you say 'um' or 'aahh' too much? Do you wave your hands? Do you speak too quickly or too softly? Do you enunciate your words well? Public speaking scares a lot of people, but the only way to take away that fear is to do more of it. Pitch to as many different people as possible and listen to their feedback about how you can improve. You have to be able to find the right words to explain your science and your product to anyone, no matter whether they have a scientific background or not. Many investors are not scientists and if they are, they may not be experts in your particular subject and technology.

Keep it simple

Do not get bogged down in jargon. Have a clear message. Explain the clinical problem in clear, simple terms then explain how your technology will solve this problem. You must show convincing scientific data but you do not have to use complicated, technical terms to explain it. If investors cannot understand what you are saying, they will not invest. Also, make sure you can talk about your science in a convincing way without sharing confidential data that might compromise your IP protection. This can be difficult and will take some practice to get right.

Tell the truth

Don't exaggerate your science or try to hide bad results. Investors are smart people and if they aren't scientists, they will have scientific advisors who will analyze your data. Don't inflate the value of your company or project revenues that you can't back up with believable numbers. Professional investors analyze companies and financial projections for a living. They will spot exaggerations immediately and if you do not tell the truth, they will not trust you. Professional relationships must be based on trust to work.

Have solid science

You need to show data to back up any claims you make. Your experiments should be well designed and well executed. Investors and pharmaceutical partners will not tolerate data that is not rigorous, controlled and reproducible. Conduct blinded studies, with positive and negative controls and enough power (*i.e.* high enough n's) to be statistically significant. And use appropriate statistical analysis, not the only test that gives you significance.

Tell a story

People will remember a story. It will resonate with them and make them want to know more. If you reel off disconnected facts and figures, your audience will stop paying attention very quickly. Present the story of why you want to solve this problem and how you are doing it.

Share your excitement

If you are excited about your science and your company, that can be infectious and make investors excited too. If you aren't excited, why should they be excited? Show them that you are passionate about what you are doing, that you truly believe you can do it and that you will do whatever it takes to achieve your goals and make your company a success. Investors are investing as much in you as they are in your technology. They have to believe that you can make your vision a reality.

Show in-depth knowledge of your industry and competitors

Some of this will come out in your pitch presentation and some won't be obvious until question time but it is very important to show investors that you know everything about your industry, your technology and your competitors.

Acknowledge risk and have a plan to mitigate it

Life science is a risky industry. Investors who regularly invest in life science companies know that. They want to know that you have considered all the different types of risk - regulatory, reimbursement, product development, customer adoption, exit - and that you have a plan to control each of these risks.

Listen

Listen to the feedback that investors give you. Take it away and use it to improve your pitch and your product development and business plans. Ask investors about what sort of deals they like to do - what types of technology, what stage, who do they want to see in a startup team? How do they want data presented? If an investor says no to your initial pitch, they may be interested at a later stage. Ask them, "Would you be interested in speaking again after we reach these milestones?" Or "What would you need to see to be interested?"

Pitch deck tips

The length of your pitch deck will depend on the length of time you are given to present. Don't guess. Ask the investors how long you have to present. If it is an hour, then prepare a 30 to 40-minute talk and allow 20 to 30 minutes for question time. If you are presenting a compelling story, you will get a lot of questions. Many investors will start asking questions on the first slide. Some like to throw you off and see how you handle this.

You can't ask investors to sign an NDA before you pitch because they won't do it. They see too many deals and don't have time to sign NDAs unless they are really serious about a company. However, you can write "Proprietary and Confidential. Prepared for [insert investment firm]. Please do not distribute." at the bottom of your slides and on any other documents you share such as your executive summary. The website Venture Hacks is full of useful advice such as this and is an excellent resource for first-time entrepreneurs.

Slide design

The same rules apply to an investor pitch as to any scientific presentation:

- Make your slides clear and simple
- Use large, simple font that anyone could read from the back of the room. Use at least 30-point font
- Keep words to a minimum
- Use graphics, graphs and pictures to illustrate your points
- Titles on each slide should be the takeaway point for that slide - sometimes people only read the title of the slide - someone should be able to click through your slides and only read the titles and still understand everything you are trying to say
- Estimate one to two minutes of speaking time per slide

Content

The content on a pitch deck should go through: *who, what, why, when, how and how much.* Start with who you are, what you are doing and why, when and how you are doing it and how much money you need to get it done.

Here is a template of recommended slides to include in your deck. You can play around with the order and the number of slides to make sure you are telling a clear, concise and compelling story within your allotted time.

1. Title slide with your company name, logo and tagline *i.e.* who you are.
2. Summary or 'key facts' slide. This is the slide version of your elevator pitch showing who you are, what

you do and how much money you are asking for. You could always use this as your title slide then investors can see it as soon as they walk in the room.

3. The problem and **pain point** you are addressing. You should talk about which disease or patient groups you are targeting, how their disease is currently managed and what key problem they face that you can solve. Make this personal. Tell a story here.
4. Your solution *i.e.* what you are doing and why. You may need more than one slide to show your data. You need to show enough data to be convincing about your mechanism of action and show how your technology is different from what is already available, but not share any non-confidential data. Include details about IP protection.
5. Why now is the right time to create this solution. You need to show that your target market is ready to adopt your technology.
6. Your team. Show that your management team and advisors have the experience, knowledge and skillset needed to execute your business plan.
7. Competitors and existing treatment/diagnosis for your disease of interest.
8. Product development plan and the road you will take to your next milestones (*i.e.* when you will be ready for a subsequent funding round).
9. Business model including your revenue model and five year projections of costs and income sources including future funding rounds, partnerships and sales.
10. Regulatory plan
11. Reimbursement plan

12. Any evidence of traction such as any customer testimonials or letters of support, or a financial summary if you have made any sales or have any partnerships in place.
13. Exit plan (in life science this is usually acquisition) with realistic valuation projections - show how much money investors could make (but be realistic and be prepared to back this up with data from comparable companies).
14. The investment opportunity *i.e.* how much money you need and in what form e.g. convertible notes and how you will use that money.
15. Summary with key takeaway points.
16. Question time.

Documents you need with your pitch

As part of the fundraising process, you will need several documents as well as your pitch deck.

Executive summary

The Executive summary is a one to two-page summary of your pitch deck. Jens Lapinski, managing director at Techstars, recommends sending a two to three-page teaser document instead of an executive summary when you first email VCs. Either way, you need a short document that summarizes who you are, what you do and why you are a good investment opportunity.

If angels and VCs like the look of your summary, they will share this document with their colleagues and ask their opinion on whether to invite you to pitch. Therefore, the point of your summary document is to outline your company as an investment opportunity and make the investors want to know more about you and see you pitch in person.

Talk to entrepreneurs who have successfully raised funding and ask if you can see their executive summaries. This will help you work out the right layout and language to use in yours. Here is a template you can use to get started.

Intro

The first paragraph has to grab the investor's attention and make them keep reading. It is essentially your elevator pitch written down.

Problem, solution and target market

The second section of your summary should define the problem you are addressing, your target market, the size of your market and your solution. Here you want to indicate that you have an interesting and novel solution to a real problem that is experienced by a large target market. Explain who your customers are—who will pay for your product or service? Patients, doctors, hospitals? Do you have any support or testimonials, or have you made any sales to these groups?

Science and Product

Summarize your core science, IP protection, and the mechanism of action of your product. Outline product development plans. All this must be non-confidential information.

Competitors

Outline the competitive landscape. What is the existing treatment or diagnostic method for your disease of interest or the problem that you are addressing? Who are your competitors? What is stopping other companies from creating a product like yours?

Offering

Explain how much money you need and what you will use it for.

Team

Show the experience that your team and your advisors have that will allow you to get your product to market and make money.

Traction

Outline any customer adoption or milestones achieved.

Financials

You may not have anything to put in this section if you are an early stage company. Report any revenue you have made and include five-year predictions for revenue, gross profit and net income (EBIDTA). EBIDTA stands for Earnings Before Interest, Taxes, Depreciation and Amortization.

Business plan

Your business plan is a blueprint for managing and operating your business. Like a product development plan and a marketing plan, this document is more for you than for any investor. You can store all the information you need to support your pitch deck in your business plan and share this document internally so that everyone in your management team agrees on business strategy, company goals and timeline.

Your pitch deck, executive summary and business plan should all be synergistic. Use your business plan to tell a story and present the business opportunity that you are offering investors. Set specific milestones and targets, outline how and when you will achieve those targets and quantify the resources you need to get there. It lays out what you need to do to build a successful business, take in revenue and increase your company valuation.

For a life science company, your business plan should include your product development plan, IP protection plan, regulatory plan, reimbursement plan and marketing and sales plans. If you prepare these all as separate documents, you can share different documents with different people instead of giving everyone a giant document with all your information. For example, an accountant may only need to see your financials and not your IP portfolio or product development plan. You can always collate all the separate documents into one large document if necessary.

Use graphics and graphs to illustrate your points wherever possible. They break up the text and draw the reader's attention.

Include any assumptions you have made and explain why you have made them. Make sure you have data to back up any claims you make in any documents that you will show investors.

Remember that even though most investors do not want to see a business plan, some will. Any documents you send to professional investors will be shared with other investors and their advisors so do not include proprietary or confidential information in your business plan or executive summary.

Technology

This section should discuss your core science, how it works and how it is different to other available technologies.

Product

This section should outline your lead product. What it is, how it works and who is your target customer.

Team

Who is in your team now? Who are your advisors? Do you have a Board of Directors? If not when will you build out this board? Project when you will need to grow your team. Who will you need to hire, when, to fill which roles and how much will this cost?

Product development plan

What are the steps you need to take to develop your product? What milestones will you meet? When? How will you meet these? What experiments will you do? Who will you partner with and when? How much money do you need? How will you use it? Where will it come from? Who will do the work? Do you have the expertise on your team already or will you need to hire people or contract out the work?

IP portfolio and strategy

Do you own all the necessary IP through patents and licenses? Do you have freedom to operate? How will you defend your IP?

Regulatory strategy

What are the requirements for the regulatory body in your country to approve your product? Are you planning on manufacturing and selling your product in any other countries? What are the regulatory requirements in these countries? What is your plan to meet these requirements? Where will your experiments be conducted? Where will your product be manufactured? How will you run clinical trials *etc.*? Will you partner? If so, with whom? Will you hire regulatory consultants? If so, when? How much will that cost? Where will you find these people?

Reimbursement strategy

Who will pay for your product? Who pays for comparable products and how much do they pay? Is it covered by Medicare or the NHS? Will private health insurers pay?

Marketing plan

Who is your target customer? How will you get to that customer? What does that customer use now to solve the problem that you aim to solve? How do they buy that product? How much does it cost? How will you switch potential customers from their current product to your product? What are your marketing milestones and timeline? I go through marketing plans in more detail in Chapter Twelve.

Sales plan

Although getting a product to market may seem very far away, it can still help to sketch out a sales plan. How much will you sell your product for? How will you sell it? Do you need to build a sales force? How will you train these people? How will you develop the marketing and sales materials to support the sales staff? Will you partner to outsource or share this with a larger company or will your company do this work yourselves?

Financial plan

This section shows any revenue or profit you have already made, as well as any costs to date and how those have been funded. It also shows how much money you need to raise and when you need to raise it to meet your milestones. Explain how you will use that money to build the value of your company and start bringing in revenue. Break down your costs into areas such as product development, administrative (the costs for staff and premises) and marketing. Make five-year projections where you estimate gross revenue, expenses, cash flow, assets and net income.

Exit strategy and industry analysis

Explain how your company fits into the industry and who is likely to want to buy you and why they are likely to buy you.

Due Diligence

If investors are interested enough in your company they will perform due diligence. They will research your company, often using outside expert advisors, to verify all your claims and make sure that you are a sound investment. They will assess you in the following areas:

1. Commercial - by analyzing the market and talking to any customers you have as well as potential customers and industry specialists
2. Financial
3. Technical (assessing the strength of your science and the risk of any regulatory hurdles) - by speaking with scientific expert/s
4. Regulatory
5. Go-to-market strategy

Keep all your data, competitive and market analysis, financials, product development, marketing and business plans and any other information you have collated in a 'data room'. Keep that data well organized. Investors could ask to see anything, so you want everything to be quick and easy to find.

If investors decide to invest and offer you a term sheet, they will also do accounting and legal due diligence. The point of due diligence is to find any reason why the investor should not give you money. Your job during this time is to provide all the information they need to convince them that you are a good investment opportunity *i.e.* that you can create a product that many people will buy and that your company will make a lot of money.

Term Sheets

Most investments rounds include more than one investor. The **lead investor** is the first person to invest in a round. If an investor wants to lead a round, they will offer you a term sheet. A term sheet sets out the basic terms and conditions of any investment offer. It is a template for the legally binding contract that you will need to sign to finalize the investment. The term sheet will include the valuation of your company, the investment amount, the percentage equity stake or value of convertible note that investors want in exchange for their money, and any anti-dilutive measures such as a cap or discount. Other investors will either offer a competing term sheet or if they want to accept the lead investor's terms, they will follow the lead as part of the syndicate.

Most professional investors will have set terms. You can negotiate but it is difficult for a first-time entrepreneur to work out which terms you can negotiate and how much you might be able to talk an investor up or down.

Ask other entrepreneurs for advice. Ask an experienced lawyer whether the terms you are given are standard and seem reasonable.

When negotiating investment terms, you need to know the market value of your company. This is much easier if you have more than one term sheet issued by different investors at the same time. That way you can compare terms and valuations.

To have a chance of having multiple term sheets issued at the same time, you must start talking to a number of different investors at the same time.

Investor term sheet basics

The language used in term sheets can be confusing for first-time entrepreneurs. Here are some of the terms that an investor may include in their term sheet.

Company valuation and investor equity

A term sheet will outline the valuation of the company and what investors get in return for their cash investment. The company valuation will dictate how much equity investors receive for their money.

For early stage companies, equity is often in the form of a convertible note, which is essentially a loan. The dollar value of the convertible note, plus any accrued interest, will be used to buy stock in the company at a later date, usually the next funding round. At this point the note will convert to equity. There are usually provisions in the term sheet to put a cap on the maximum share value at which the note will convert to equity. This means that even if investors value your share price at $2.00 per share in the next round, if you have a cap of $1.50 per share price, investors from the first round essentially get a 50c per share discount. These sorts of terms are to *prevent equity dilution*, so that the value of an early stage investment isn't diluted when you raise the next funding round (see more about equity dilution in Chapter Thirteen). Investors want this sort of benefit as a reward for taking on the risk of early stage investment.

In later stage rounds, investment money immediately buys investors equity in the form of shares. The share price is set based on the company valuation at each funding round. This is decided after a discussion between the entrepreneurs and all investors and must increase with each funding round to provide a return on investment for the original investors. If share price goes down in a subsequent round, it is called a **down round**. As well as a conversion cap, investors will include other anti-dilution protection to prevent them from losing money in the event of a down round.

Anti-dilution protection

Anti-dilution provisions are added to term sheets to protect investors if a company is valued at a lower valuation in a future round (a down round) and to mitigate the dilution that occurs when new shares are issued in each subsequent funding round.

As I discussed in Chapter Eleven, investors usually want to be issued preferred shares. They may want convertible preferred shares, which means that when there is a liquidation event (*e.g.* the company is sold) the preferred shares convert to a predetermined number of common shares, either at the share price at the time of liquidation or at a predetermined price point.

A **full-ratchet** adjustment means that in the event of a down round, all of an investor's preferred shares will convert to common shares at the new lower share price, instead of at the higher previous price. This means that the original investor's money is now worth more common shares to compensate for the lower price of the shares. For example, if share value was $2.00 in a Series A round, but dropped to $1.00 in a Series B round, and an investor included a full-ratchet adjustment provision in the term sheet, his or her preferred shares would now convert to common shares at $1.00 instead of $2.00. Therefore, each of the original investor's preferred shares would now be able to convert to two common shares instead of one at a liquidation event, thus maintaining the value of their investment.

> ***Watch out for full ratchet***
>
> *Full-ratchet adjustment clauses can make companies less attractive to future investors because the company and future investor will carry all the risk of any drop in valuation. You should always try to negotiate to replace any full-ratchet terms with weighted average terms.*

Weighted average anti-dilution protection may be used in new financing rounds to mitigate the dilution that occurs when new shares are issued. Weighted average protection recalculates the rate at which preferred shares will convert to common shares.

Narrow-based weighted average protection only affects outstanding preferred shares in each funding round *i.e.* shares that have already been issued before a new funding round. It does not affect the conversion rate of any new shares issued during the new round.

Broad-based weighted average protection affects all equity *i.e.* all outstanding shares and all newly issued shares.

Type of stock

Investors will specify the type of stock they wish to receive in exchange for their investment (see Chapter Eleven for an explanation of stock classes). They will usually ask for preferred stock which comes with certain benefits such as voting rights, and dividend and liquidation privileges *i.e.* preferred stock holders receive their share of any dividends and any proceeds from the sale of the company before common stock holders. Preferred shares may be **cumulative**, meaning that if a company cannot afford to pay dividends one year, this value will accumulate until the company can pay. They may also be **convertible,** so they can be converted to a pre-determined number of common shares at a future date, usually a subsequent funding round. They may also be **callable** or **redeemable** which means that the company may or will buy them back at a fixed price at or by a certain date or milestone.

Liquidation preference

If this isn't part of the preferred stock rights, investors will include a separate clause stating that they have the right to be paid first in any liquidation event e.g. when the company is sold. This right usually extends to the value of the invested capital, so that investors will at least get their money back, even if they don't make any money on the investment.

Participation rights

Participation rights mean that once investors have recouped their initial investment, they are also allowed to receive their share of any remaining proceeds from the sale of the company.

For example, if preferred stock holders (investors) invested $2 million in your company in exchange for 40% equity, they will have the right to receive at least $2 million when the company is sold. If your company sells for $5 million, preferred stock holders automatically receive $2 million. If they also have participation rights, then they also receive 40% of the remaining $3 million, which is $1.2 million. So only $1.8 million of the proceeds will then be divided among common shareholders.

Participation rights make it harder for common stock holders (including founders) to receive their share of any proceeds. Therefore, try to negotiate a cap to participation rights for preferred stock holders.

Option pool

Many term sheets will include an option pool, which is a pool of shares set aside to compensate directors, management, employees and consultants (see more on options in Chapter Eleven). Make sure you understand whether investors want the option pool to be calculated based on the pre-money valuation of your company or the post-money valuation of your company. If it is on the pre-money valuation, that means that founders and existing investors will have the value of their shares diluted when any new option pool shares are issued. If it is on post-money valuation that means that all investors, including those in the new round, will be diluted. Therefore, issuing an option pool based on post-money valuation is a better option for founders and existing investors because the value of their stock will be less diluted. However, it is a worse option for new investors because they will have to share the dilution - something they don't want to do.

Board seat

Most VC investors will ask for a seat on your Board of Directors as that gives them some control of company decisions. While early stage companies can benefit greatly from the wisdom and business acumen of an experienced investor, you want to limit the number of board seats occupied by investors. You want to make sure that investors don't hold more seats than founders, or people who are on the founders' side. Your board needs to be balanced, in terms of the decision-making power held by founders and investors. Therefore, you do not want to give a seat to every investor in a multi-investor round.

Tranches

Some term sheets will offer investment in **tranches** or stages. This means that only part of the total investment money will be available to you at the start and the rest will become available at certain dates or when you reach certain milestones. Investors like tranches because it limits their financial risk. However, from the entrepreneur point of view, it is always better to have all of the money at the beginning so you can use it as necessary.

Buyback rights

This is the right to buy shares from any investors who are exiting. This means that any investor who wants to sell their shares must first offer them to anyone with buyback rights (usually founders and other investors), before offering them to others. Always include buyback rights for founders. Most VCs will also ask for these.

Drag-along rights

Drag-along rights allow major shareholders to force minor shareholders to agree to the sale of a company.

Tag-along rights

Tag-along rights give minor shareholders the right to sell their shares if a major shareholder sells their stake in the company. Tag-along rights allow minor shareholders to become part of the transaction negotiated by the major shareholder. This means they can sell their shares at the same time for the same value.

Protective provisions

These give investors the right to veto certain company decisions such as preventing the company from borrowing more than a certain amount of money or restricting the number of authorized shares that you can issue in exchange for funding.

Further Resources

Free online resources where you can find more information about the concepts outlined in this chapter.

7 Keys to a Compelling Executive Summary That Wins Over Investors:
https://www.entrepreneur.com/article/247312#

A Technical Due Diligence Framework for Early Stage Startups: https://medium.com/point-nine-news/a-technical-due-diligence-framework-for-early-stage-startups-c24d5408256e

Anatomy of an (Un)fundable Startup:
http://venturehacks.com/articles/unfundable-startup

Are You Ready for Funding? The Anatomy of a Future Startup Unicorn: https://medium.com/@founding/are-you-ready-for-funding-the-anatomy-of-a-future-startup-unicorn-7e5739e1734e

Jens Lapinski's VC fundraising manual:
https://jenslapinski.com/2008/06/20/vc-fund-raising-manual/

Sample Term Sheet (from MaRS):
https://www.marsdd.com/mars-library/term-sheet-template-for-angel-or-venture-capital-investors/

StartupGrind Startup Pitch Decks:
https://medium.com/startup-grind/all-the-public-startup-pitch-decks-in-one-place-7d3ddff33bdc

Term Sheets: The Definitive Guide for Entrepreneurs: https://www.capshare.com/blog/term-sheets-guide/

The Art of the Executive Summary (by Guy Kawasaki): https://guykawasaki.com/the_art_of_the_-3/

The Perfect Executive Summary (by venture capitalist Andy Clapp): https://venturefund.wordpress.com/the-perfect-executive-summary-still-looking-for-it/

VC-List Startup Investment Due Diligence Checklist: http://vc-list.com/startup-investment-due-diligence-checklist/

What is Weighted Average Anti-Dilution Protection: http://www.startupcompanylawyer.com/2007/08/04/what-is-weighted-average-anti-dilution-protection/

Conclusion

While this book is meant as a guide for first-time entrepreneurs, the only real way to learn how to be an entrepreneur is to become one. Drew Titmarsh is an academic scientist-turned CEO. He co-founded Scaled Biolabs, a company with technology that allows researchers to conduct thousands of cell culture experiments simultaneously.

Drew's advice is to start as early as possible. "The earlier you can start, the further along you will be," he said. "Not doing it means you'll be nowhere. Forget the academic stuff - that's probably already been dealt with sufficiently in your past work - and focus on solving a problem for someone."

Founding a life science company gives you the chance to change the health and lives of millions of people around the world. This sort of dream is why many of us studied science or medicine in the first place.

It takes an exorbitant amount of hard work to found and run a company. It is a rollercoaster ride, with exhilarating highs and devastating lows. You have to convince yourself and the world that you are creating something of value, a product or service that will solve a big problem.

You will have many sleepless nights and your friends and family may think you are crazy. But for natural entrepreneurs, the challenges that come with starting a company are thrilling. Every day is different. Every day you are solving problems, meeting goals and climbing the mountain towards first revenue or a successful exit.

As Ravata Solutions CEO, Arshia Firouzi, told me, "This is the most fun I've ever had doing anything."

If you found this book useful, please consider leaving an Amazon review. I have published independently to keep the price as low as possible. The only way people can find out about new independent books is by referral and reviews.

Acknowledgements

I would like to thank all the entrepreneurs who shared their stories with me and allowed me to use their quotes in this book. Many of those quotes came from interviews I did while working at Life Science Network. You can find the full interviews at: www.lifesciencenetwork.com.

I also want to thank you for reading and wish you the best of luck on your entrepreneurship journey.

Glossary

A list of basic business terms that appeared throughout this book. Understanding these terms will help you communicate with advisors, mentors and investors, as well as read articles and books on entrepreneurship.

A

A/B testing: A simple experiment where you test two different marketing conditions to see which performs better.

Accredited investors: The guidelines on who can become an accredited investor vary from country to country but in general, you have to meet certain earning or asset thresholds to be accredited. In the US, you must have earned at least $200,000 per year for the past two years or have over $1 million in assets, excluding your primary residence.

Acquisition: When a company is bought by another company. **Mergers** (when two companies merge to form a single corporate entity) and acquisitions are the most common form of **exit** for life science companies.

Advisory board: A group of domain experts who help you make business and scientific decisions for your company.

AgTech: Agriculture technology companies.

Angel investor: High net-worth individual who invests his or her own money. **Venture capitalists**, in contrast, manage investment funds, and therefore, invest other people's money.

Anti-dilution protection: Clauses in an investment agreement that aim to limit how much existing shareholders' ownership in the company is diluted when new investment is taken on. In each new funding round, new shares are issued which increases the total number of company shares. This means that existing shareholders effectively own less of the company.

Available market: The percentage of your target market that you can reach with your marketing.

B

Bayh-Dole Act: US legislation passed in 1980 that allows universities and non-profit research institutes to own any technology arising from federally-funded research at their facilities. This law requires universities and institutes to patent any useful inventions that they own and to license that technology to interested commercial partners. In Europe, universities and research institutes may have similar intellectual property rights in place.

Best-in-class: A drug that works in a similar way to the market leader but has better pharmacokinetics.

Board of Directors: A group of people legally liable for the actions of the company who have voting rights in any important company decisions.

Breakthrough therapy: An FDA term to describe drug candidates that treat a serious condition and for which preliminary data shows the drug is substantially superior to current drugs in one or more **clinically significant endpoints**.

Burn rate: The number of customers who stop using your product or service. Also called **drop-out rate.**

Business development: Developing partnerships to help your company grow. This includes corporate partners, investors, supporters such as patient advocacy groups and large or corporate customers. Both marketing and business development will find and nurture **leads** (potential customers) and pass them to the sales team when the potential customers are ready to buy.

Business-to-Business (B2B): A business model selling to other businesses.

Business-to-Consumer (B2C): A business model selling to individual consumers, not businesses.

Buyback rights: The right to buy shares from any investors who are exiting. This means that any investor who wants to sell their shares must first offer them to anyone with buyback rights (usually founders and other investors), before offering them to others. Always include buyback rights for founders. Most VCs will also ask for these.

Buying cycle: The stages that a prospective customer goes through before buying a product. These stages are: being unaware of the problem; knowing about the problem; looking for solutions; comparing options and deciding to buy. Also called a **sales funnel**.

C

C Corp: The standard corporate structure in the US. C Corp founders and shareholders do not have to be US citizens or permanent residents, although US law prohibits people from certain countries from owning US assets. In a C Corp, the business must file its own tax return and company profits are taxed at the corporate tax rate. If any of the profits go to shareholders as dividends, they are also taxed at the dividend rate. This double taxation is avoided in S Corps. C Corps can issue multiple share types and can create stock options to incentivize employees.

Call to action: A call on every piece of marketing material where you tell the reader/viewer what it is that you want them to do, for example, sign up to an email list or click through to another webpage.

Capitalization (Cap) table: A cap table is a running list of shareholders, shares and financing rounds. Every time you take investment or issue shares, you need to enter that transaction into your cap table.

Class I medical devices: Devices with minimal potential to harm a user *e.g.* an elastic bandage. In the US, 95% of Class I devices are exempt from premarket submission, which means that you do not need FDA approval before marketing your device. However, for the other 5%, you will need to submit a premarket notification, also called a 510(k). Every medical device sold in Europe must have a **Conformité Européenne (CE) mark** showing that it complies with the essential requirements of European health, safety and environmental protection laws.

Class II medical device: Devices with some potential for harm *e.g.* an electric wheelchair. For most Class II devices in the US, you must submit a premarket notification 510(k) or a **premarket approval application (PMA)**. Every medical device sold in Europe must have a Conformité Européenne (CE) mark showing that it complies with the essential requirements of European health, safety and environmental protection laws.

Class III medical device: Devices that support or sustain life or prevent the impairment of human health. This includes devices such as surgical implants. In the US, a **premarket approval (PMA) application** must be submitted for all Class III medical devices. The application must include all preclinical and clinical data. Every medical device sold in Europe must have a Conformité Européenne (CE) mark showing that it complies with the essential requirements of European health, safety and environmental protection laws.

Clinical Trial Authorization (CTA): Approval from a relevant European regulatory body to conduct a clinical trial in a European country. You must receive a CTA from each European country in which you wish to conduct any trials. You can submit clinical trials through the Common European Submission Portal (CESP), provided by the Heads of Medicines Agency (HMA). The CESP is a single platform that allows you to communicate with regulatory agencies across Europe.

Clinically significant endpoint: An outcome (symptom, sign or laboratory/diagnostic value) that indicates whether a trialed drug or device is safe or effectively diagnoses or treats a certain disease condition.

Common or ordinary shares: These shares have one vote per share, equal dividend rights and no priority for a cash return when the company exits.

Company mission: An internal statement reminding all company management, advisors, investors, mentors and employees what your core mission is and what you are all working to achieve. It is a statement about what your company does. You should use your company mission to draft company goals and create your company culture. Everything you do as a leader in your company should stay true to your company mission.

Company vision: Explains what you want your company to become *e.g.* the leading cancer diagnostic company or improve the lives of all Type 2 Diabetes patients.

Competitive advantage: Features of your product, service or company that make you better than competitors. Also called your **point of difference** or **unique selling point**.

Confidential disclosure agreement (CDA): A legally binding document that prevents the signee (advisor, mentor, investor, employee or consultant) from disclosing or using information about your company. Also called a **non-disclosure agreement (NDA).**

Conformité Européenne (CE) mark: This mark is required on any device sold in the EU and shows the device complies with the essential requirements of European health, safety and environmental protection laws. This essentially means that the device works as you intend it to work and that any benefits outweigh any risks to patients.

Convertible Note: A loan given to companies by investors in exchange for the rights to buy equity in the company at a future point, usually during the next funding round. The dollar value of the convertible note plus any accrued interest will be used to buy stock in the company at a later date i.e. will be converted to equity. There are usually provisions in the term sheet to put a cap on the maximum share value at which the note will convert to equity. This means that even if investors value your share price at $2.00 per share in the next round, if you have a cap of $1.50 per share price, investors from the first round essentially get a 50c per share discount.

Conversion rate: The number of potential customers who buy your product or service and turn into customers.

Crowdfunding: Where individuals or businesses use an online platform to raise money from a large number of people - a 'crowd'.

Customer: Customers are the people who pay for your product or service and **end-users** are the people who use it. They are not always the same.

Customer lifetime value: An estimate of the net profit that a customer will bring your company over the lifetime of their relationship with you.

Customer persona: A description of your target customer based on customer interviews and research on customer spending habits: their disposable income; what they purchase and how; the price bracket in which they will buy an equivalent product and their design preferences. Also called a customer avatar.

D

Digital marketing: Any marketing through digital channels including the web and mobile phones.

Direct competitors: All other companies creating products or services that solve the same problem for the same target market as your product or service.

Direct marketing: Selling straight to customers, for example email marketing and social media marketing.

Distribution channels: The ways in which you make a product or service available to customers. These can be direct or indirect. Also known as **marketing channels**.

Drag-along rights: A clause in an investment agreement that allows major shareholders to force minor shareholders to agree to the sale of a company.

Due diligence: The background research that an investor conducts before deciding whether or not to invest in a company.

E

Earned media: Media that you did not pay for and you did not create. It is media created by an independent person like a journalist. It is often the most powerful form of media because it comes with inherent **third party validation** *i.e.* someone other than you is talking about your company or product and this is always more believable than when you talk about yourself.

EBIDTA: Earnings Before Interest, Taxes, Depreciation and Amortization. This term is often used to describe net profits when speaking with investors.

End-user: End-users are the people who use your product or service and customers are the people who pay for it. They are not always the same.

Equity or debt crowdfunding: When companies use a crowdfunding platform to raise money from many different investors in return for equity or as a loan.

European Authorised Representative: A person within the European Economic Area (EEA) appointed to help a manufacturer outside of the EEA liaise with European regulatory bodies.

Exit: In investment terms, an exit is when investors and/or founders take their money out of a company. This happens when a company is bought by a bigger company, as a **merger** or **acquisition**, or floats on a public stock exchange, through an **initial public offering** (IPO). The most common exit for life science startups is acquisition.

F

Family office: An office that manages money for one or more wealthy families. There are more than 3,000 of these offices around the world managing $4 trillion. They can be either single-family offices (SFOs) or multi-family offices (MFOs).

Fast track FDA review: Accelerated review of drugs that treat serious conditions or fill an unmet medical need such as Alzheimer's disease, heart failure or cancer.

Feasibility trial: Preliminary safety and performance study of a medical device in 10 to 30 patients with the target disease. Part of the US regulatory pathway for medical devices.

First-in-class: A drug with a new mode of action to treat a particular disease.

First-in-human (FIH) trial: The first time a new drug candidate or medical device has been clinically trialed in humans.

Follow-on funding: When an investment firm that has already invested in your company chooses to invest in a subsequent round.

Founders' shares: Shares issued at the time of incorporation for a nominal price - often $0.001 per share. These are usually common shares, although they can be preferred. Founders may choose to confer specific rights to this class of shares. Be wary of doing this as it may make investors less inclined to invest in your company. Founders' shares are often vested, so founders will receive a certain percentage of shares over a period of time or when the company meets certain milestones.

Freedom to operate: The legal right, through intellectual property ownership, to execute your business and product development plans.

G

General Data Protection Regulation (GDPR): Legislation that harmonizes data privacy laws in European countries. It regulates the collection and use of any personal data to sell goods or services to citizens of EU member countries. GDPR rules apply to all companies using the personal data of EU citizens, even if those companies are based outside of the EU.

Go/no-go decision: A decision whether or not to continue with your current product development and business plans. Entrepreneurs must constantly assess whether they are developing the right product or application and building the right business to be profitable. You should constantly be making 'go/no-go' decisions.

Good Clinical Practice (GCP): A set of international standards, both scientific and ethical, that outline how to design, record and report clinical trials on humans. These standards are based on the World Medical Association's Declaration of Helsinki which was first published in 1964 with the goal of protecting any humans who take part in clinical research.

Good Manufacturing Practice (GMP): A set of guidelines covering the production of drugs, devices or food for humans. These guidelines are designed to ensure all approved products are safe for human use. The guidelines cover all aspects of production including the starting materials, premises, equipment, staff training and hygiene, and packing of the final product. It is essential that you document all procedures used at every step during production to prove that you have followed GMP. The exact documentation required will vary from country to country. Also called Quality System (QS) Regulation.

H

Health Information Technology for Economic and Clinical Health (HITECH): Part of the American Recovery and Reinvestment Act. HITECH regulates the use of health information technology such as electronic health records.

Health Insurance Portability and Accountability Act of 1996 (HIPAA): Legislation regulating the collection, storage, use and disclosure of Protected Health Information - all information about health, healthcare and healthcare payment.

Humanitarian Device Exemption: FDA designation for devices designed to diagnose and/or treat orphan diseases (diseases or conditions that affect 4,000 or fewer patients each year in the US). This must be approved by the FDA before you can market your device.

I

Indirect competitors: Companies creating products or services that solve a similar problem for the same target market as your product or service.

Indirect marketing: Selling through wholesalers or distributers, for example small antibody manufacturers may sell their products to a large life science company like Thermo Fisher rather than trying to sell directly to consumers.

Initial Public Offering (IPO): The first time a company publicly offers shares by listing on a public stock market (floating).

Investigational Device Exemption (IDE): This allows a new medical device to be used in a clinical study for the purpose of collecting data on the safety and effectiveness of the device. This exemption requires that any investigators receive hands-on training in how to use the device before starting the trial. Manufacturers must apply to the FDA's Center for Devices and Radiological Health for an IDE before performing any clinical trials of devices in humans in the US.

Investigational Medicinal Product (IMP): A drug candidate in Europe that has not yet been approved by the European Medicines Agency.

Investigational New Drug (IND) application: An application to the FDA requesting the right to conduct any clinical trials of new drug candidates in humans.

K

Key opinion leader: Expert in his or her field who influences the opinions and practice of other professionals.

Key Performance Indicators (KPIs): Metrics that allow you to measure the progress of your product development and marketing plans.

Keywords: The words or phrases that people use when searching the internet. You want to pick the keywords with the most traffic but the least competition. Once you have chosen keywords, you should include them in your website pages and blog posts to improve your website ranking in search engines for those terms.

L

Laboratory-Developed Test (LDT): An *in vitro* diagnostic test that has been developed, manufactured and used within the same laboratory. If any of the development, manufacturing or use has been conducted outside of one laboratory, the test cannot be considered an LDT. LDTs do not currently need regulatory approval but the FDA is setting up new guidelines to cover this class of devices.

Lead investor: The first investor to invest in a funding round.

License: The right to use intellectual property owned by someone else. There are three main types of license: exclusive, sole and non-exclusive. Licenses can also be world-wide or restricted to one or more countries. An exclusive license gives a licensee the exclusive rights to use the IP covered by the license. In the case of an exclusive license, the IP owner can no longer use that IP. A sole license also gives a single licensee rights to use the IP, however, the licensor retains the right to also use the IP. A non-exclusive license means that other people can also acquire a license to use that same IP.

Limited Liability Company (LLC): An organizational structure in the US that limits the personal financial liability of owners and has flexible taxation rules - you can elect to be taxed as sole proprietor, partnership, S Corp or C Corp. LLC may be the best choice for you if your company does not yet need outside investment and is losing money. However, you can't easily offer stock options to incentivize employees or contractors if you are an LLC. Also, you can't issue shares in an LLC. You need shares to exchange for investment. Therefore, investors do not like to invest in LLCs, they prefer C Corps. For these reasons, some entrepreneurs choose to start as an LLC to protect themselves from personal liability, then change to a C Corp when they start to look for outside investment.

M

Market penetrance: How many people will use your product instead of competing products. This depends on the visibility of your product *i.e.* how well you market it.

Marketing: Building and delivering an application to a customer. It encompasses all communication with actual and potential customers.

Marketing Authorization Application (MAA): An application submitted to the European Medicines Agency requesting approval to market an investigational medicinal product (new drug candidate).

Marketing channels: The ways in which you make a product or service available to customers. These can be direct or indirect. Also known as **distribution channels**.

Marketing strategy: A big picture statement about how you will use marketing to achieve your sales and business goals. If your business goal is to develop the leading multiple sclerosis pharmaceutical then your marketing strategy may be to reach multiple sclerosis patients and healthcare providers across the US (or Europe or Japan).

Marketing tactics: Specific methods you use to execute your marketing strategy such as create a twitter account and follow anyone who comes up under the search for 'multiple sclerosis' or attend the MS Frontiers conference in the UK and talk to at least five healthcare providers about how they treat patients and what they would like to see in a new product.

Material Transfer Agreement (MTA): An agreement between labs sharing materials and reagents. An MTA should clearly state who is using what and who owns any intellectual property resulting from the use of these materials.

Medtech: Medical device and diagnostic companies.

Merger: When two companies merge to become one corporate identity. Mergers and **acquisitions** (when a company is bought by another company) are the most common form of **exit** for life science companies.

Minimally acceptable product description: Outlines the minimum safety and efficacy benchmarks that your product must reach to continue development.

Minimum viable product: An early prototype or early proof-of-concept studies in cells or animal models that validate your product development plan.

N

New Drug Application (NDA): An application submitted to the FDA to request approval of a new drug candidate. NDAs include all data collected from clinical trials, along with all preclinical data and labeling information to the FDA.

Non-assert letter: A letter from your institution stating they will not contest ownership of your intellectual property.

Non-compete clause: A clause in an employee contract or an employment contract with a contractor that prevents that party from working for a competitor for a certain amount of time following completion of their work or termination of their employment.

Non-Disclosure Agreement (NDA): A legally binding document that prevents the signee (advisor, mentor, investor, employee or consultant) from disclosing or using information about your company. Also called a **confidential disclosure agreement (CDA)**.

Non-voting shares: Either common or preferred shares that do not carry any voting rights.

Notified Body: Independent company designated by an EU member state to oversee testing of medical devices. There are more than 50 notified bodies and companies are free to choose any of them to test their devices.

O

Obtainable market: The percentage of your target market that will buy your product or use your service.

Outsource: Pay external contractors or companies to conduct work for you.

Owned media: Any media that you create on a channel that you own. This includes any content on your website, email marketing, eBooks, white papers, videos and social media posts.

P

Paid media: Any media you pay for. This includes print, TV and radio advertisements, pay per click ads, social media ads and promoted posts, search engine ads and promoted listings and some contributed articles or editorials in trade publications or other media outlets.

Pain point: The key problem that your target customer has that your product or service solves.

Patent: The right to exclude others from making, using, offering for sale, or selling an invention.

Patent analysis: Searching national patent databases, as well as all published scientific literature and conference proceedings, to check whether similar technology has already been patented for the same applications that you wish to cover under your patent.

Patent claims: All of the intended uses of your technology that you want to protect.

Patent Cooperation Treaty (PCT): An agreement that allows you to file one international patent application that simultaneously seeks patent protection in any or all of the 152 countries that have signed the treaty (these countries are called contracting states).

Phase I Clinical Trial (Safety): Researchers test the safety and side effects of an experimental drug in 20 to 100 healthy volunteers for the first time. This data helps to establish a safe dose range in humans and to understand the pharmacokinetics (absorption, distribution, metabolism and excretion) of the drug in humans.

Phase II Clinical Trial (Proof of Concept): Researchers further test the efficacy and safety of the experimental drug in up to several hundred people with a specific disease or condition. This data must show that the drug interacts with its target and improves one or more clinically relevant outcomes in a patient population. It also helps to establish the best dose range and dosing regimen and to discover common side effects.

Phase III Clinical Trial (Evidence for Regulatory Approval): Researchers test the effectiveness, safety and side effects of the experimental drug in 300 to 3,000 people and compare this data with placebo and/or with the standard of care for that disease.

Phase IV Clinical Trial (Post-marketing Safety): The drug has now been approved by the FDA and marketed and Phase IV trials monitor drug safety and risks in several thousand volunteers. This may include trialing the drug in children or other new patient populations.

Pitch deck: The PowerPoint or keynote slide presentation you use when pitching to investors.

Pipeline: Comprises any products a company is developing. The products can be at difference stages of development and have different indications.

Pivot: A fundamental change in your business. This change can be related to your product, your target customer or the way your business is set up.

Pivotal trial: Efficacy and adverse effects study of a medical device in 150 to 300 patients. This follows a **feasibility trial** in the US regulatory pathway for medical devices.

Platform: A platform is an ecosystem or a system that connects people or allows people to make products.

Point of difference: Features of your product, service or company that make you better than competitors. Also called your **competitive advantage** or **unique selling point**.

Post-approval trials: Long-term collection of safety, performance and side effect data for marketed medical devices in the US. These trials are conducted after a device is approved by the FDA to be marketed.

Preferred or preference shares: Have preferential dividend rights or guaranteed dividend amounts and priority for a cash return when the company exits. This means that preferred shareholders are paid first both in annual dividends and on exit. Preferred shares may be cumulative, meaning that if a company cannot afford to pay dividends one year, this value will accumulate until the company can pay. They may also be convertible, so they can be converted to a pre-determined number of common shares at a future date, usually a subsequent funding round. They may also be callable or redeemable which means that the company may or will buy them back at a fixed price at or by a certain date or milestone.

Pre-money valuation: The value put on your company before you receive any investment or financing.

Post-money valuation: The value put on your company after you close a funding round. This will equal the pre-money valuation plus the dollar amount of any newly invested money.

Price advantage: A competitive advantage by which your product or service is cheaper than competitors.

Prior art: All information published or publically disclosed about an invention or similar inventions before a patent application is submitted. If prior art exists for your invention, it may mean that your invention is not 'new' in the legal sense and so is not patentable.

Priority date: The official date from which you are legally recognized as having the right to exclude others from using and commercializing your technology.

Priority review: Cuts FDA review time from ten months to six months. You can apply for priority review if you have evidence that your drug outperforms those on the market by being more effective, having fewer or less severe side effects or improving patient compliance.

Product: A discrete stand-alone entity that can bought or sold.

Product/market fit: A product that solves a real need for a large market.

Public relations (PR): Creating awareness of your company and product by communicating with, and building relationships with, all audiences other than customers. This includes investors, partners, employees, end-users and the general public.

Q

Quality system (QS) regulation: A set of guidelines covering the production of drugs, devices or food for humans and is designed to ensure all approved products are safe for human use. The guidelines cover all aspects of production including the starting materials, premises, equipment, staff training and hygiene, and packing of the final product. It is essential that you document all procedures used at every step during production to prove that you have followed the regulations. The exact documentation required will vary from country to country. Also called **Good manufacturing practice (GMP)**.

R

Reimbursement: Whether a payer (a health insurance company or national healthcare system) will pay for your product or service.

Reward or donation crowdfunding: A funding method where a crowd of people give money as a donation or purchase a product or service that has not yet been developed. Most people raise only small amounts of money in the range of $1,000 to $10,000 through these crowdfunding sites.

S

Sales funnel: The stages that a prospective customer goes through before buying a product. These stages are: being unaware of the problem; knowing about the problem; looking for solutions; comparing options and deciding to buy. Also called a **buying cycle**.

S Corp: A corporate structure with special tax status. Choosing to be an S Corp will help you to avoid the double taxation you will face as a C Corp. However, the structure of an S corporation puts restrictions on your equity and capital structure and makes it hard to take outside investment. An S Corp can only have up to 100 shareholders and these can only be 'natural persons' who are US citizens or green card holders. This means no businesses, institutional investors or foreign investors can provide funding. Also, you can only have one type of stock, which means you cannot issue preferred shares to investors. Many investors will refuse to fund companies if they cannot have preferred shares.

Sales: Closing the actual transaction where money is exchanged for goods or services. Sales staff will have specific sales targets.

Service: A service provides value or creates products for people.

Share register: A record of the number and classes of all shares you have issued as well as details on all shareholders - their names and addresses, dates they acquired shares and how many shares of each class they own.

Sponsored research agreement: If a company sponsors academic research, this agreement may give the sponsoring company the first right to refuse licensing any resulting IP or they may have a time window in which they can negotiate to license any technology.

Stock options: Give recipients the right to purchase shares for a set price (the exercise price). Stock options can be used to incentivize employees, directors and consultants in place of cash remuneration. Like stock, options can be vested so they will only become available after an employee or consultant has worked for the company for a certain amount of time or has achieved certain milestones. Options can be very valuable if the market value of the company stock becomes much higher than the exercise price. If you want to be able to issue stock options, you will need to set aside an option pool when you divide up the equity among founders. Many people choose to keep 10-20% of company shares aside as options.

SWOT analysis: Analysis of the Strengths, Weaknesses, Opportunities and Threats of your company. It makes you look at whether your products really are different and better than competitors.

T

Tag-along rights: Give minor shareholders the right to sell their shares if a major shareholder sells their stake in the company. Tag-along rights allow minor shareholders to become part of the transaction negotiated by the major stakeholder. This means they can sell their shares at the same time for the same value.

Target Product Profile (TPP): Outlines the ideal characteristics of your product, including how it compares with the current standard of care. If your product is not better than the current standard of care, it is unlikely to be approved by regulatory bodies. A TPP also lists the studies required to show that your product meets minimum safety and efficacy benchmarks.

Term sheet: A document that sets out the basic terms and conditions of any investment offer. It is a template for the legally binding contract that you will need to sign to finalize the investment.

Third party validation: When someone other than you recommends or positively reviews your company or product. This is always more believable than when you talk about yourself.

Total addressable market (TAM): The revenue you would earn if you could reach 100% of your target market.

Traction: In the words of Naval Ravikant, CEO and co-founder of AngelList, startup traction means "quantitative evidence of market demand". It means showing that customers want your product or service.

Trade secret: Company information that is protected by non-disclosure agreements, secure storage and limited sharing rather than by patents.

Trademark: Legal protection for a sign, design or expression that prevents others from using that property without your permission.

Tranches: Some term sheets will offer investment in tranches or stages. This means that only part of the total investment money will be available to you at the start and the rest will become available at certain dates or when you reach certain milestones. Investors like tranches because it limits their financial risk. However, from the entrepreneur point of view, it is always better to have all of the money at the beginning so you can use it as necessary.

U

Unique selling point: Features of your product, service or company that make you better than competitors. Also called your **value proposition** or your **point of difference**.

V

Valuation: What investors believe your company is worth or will be worth in the near future. A **pre-money valuation** is the value put on your company before you receive any investment or financing. A **post-money valuation** is the valuation of your company after an investment round. Valuations of early stage life science companies are usually $5 to 10 million or less.

Value proposition: An external statement telling the world why they should buy your product or use your service.

Venture capitalists: Investors who manage investment funds, and therefore, invest other people's money.

Venture philanthropy: Financial support of drug or device development programs from patient advocacy groups or other philanthropic organizations in exchange for equity or a share in the royalties.

Vesting: When founders, employees or consultants earn the right to their company shares over time. Offering shares under a vesting schedule can help ensure people continue to work hard to grow the company and earn their shares.

Virtual company: A company in which a core team essentially project manages the company and outsources all work to different contractors, contract research organizations and consultants.

Made in the USA
Monee, IL
11 February 2022

91085807R00168